SILEN

SILENT HEROES
The Story of the SAS

GRAEME STEWART

MICHAEL O'MARA BOOKS LIMITED

First published in Great Britain in 1997 by
Michael O'Mara Books Limited
9 Lion Yard, Tremadoc Road
London SW4 7NQ

A CIP catalogue record for this book is available from the
British Library

ISBN 1-85479-635-6

1 3 5 7 9 10 8 6 4 2

Designed and typeset by Martin Bristow
Printed and bound by Cox & Wyman, Reading

CONTENTS

AUTHOR'S PREFACE

Most people in today's Western world have heard of the Special Air Service Regiment (SAS) with its origins in the North African deserts of the Second World War. The younger reader is most likely to remember those dramatic images on television in May 1980 when men clad from head to toe in black stormed the Iranian Embassy in London, killing terrorists as efficiently as a surgeon with a scalpel, and freeing their terrified hostages. The BBC interrupted a John Wayne western to show live pictures of the assault by real-life James Bonds, the first time a modern anti-terrorist unit had been seen in action in Britain. For a few brief minutes, the nation held its breath.

In recent times numerous books and films have appeared recounting the history and the exploits of 'the Regiment', as the SAS is known to the men who have won the sand-coloured beret with its flaming sword badge. Anyone attempting to write a factual account of their activities and their methods is faced with a difficult task because of the code of secrecy that surrounds SAS operations and the preferred anonymity of its soldiers. The Ministry of Defence in London never officially discusses special forces operations, past or present.

The wartime SAS was a different organization from today's regiment although its ideology and the element of secrecy was always there. In today's rapidly changing military world where one man or woman armed with a shoulder-fired missile can destroy a multi-million pound fighter aircraft, generals and politicians who direct wars have finally realized the value of the well-trained, highly motivated and superbly equipped infantry soldier. To understand what makes Britain's secret warriors 'tick', some understanding of their ideology is required. One thing is certain, whatever faces today's soldier has undoubtedly been experienced by others who went before him. Maintaining stamina and courage in battle, or the nail-biting hours leading up to it, has daunted the toughest of men since the days of Genghis Khan or the Roman legions. Dealing with white-out blizzard conditions in the South Atlantic or walking through the deserts of Arabia where men can die of hypothermia or dehydration are just daily problems for the soldier to resolve.

In my conversations with the men who have served in 22 Special Air Service Regiment, several things remain constant. Almost all are naturally friendly and warm-hearted, interested in you as a person and, should one need their help, be it to change a wheel without a jack or rescue someone from an angry crowd carrying machetes, they know how to do it. Whether they will or not, usually depends on whether they like you. Most are family men, though broken marriages are not uncommon. They rarely look like thugs, with one or two notable exceptions. Most, apart from the odd officer, would feel quite at home on a building site, though they would probably complain to the foreman about pay and conditions. All are naturally good at working with their hands. Their capacity for alcohol is legendary, though most remain exceptionally fit, if sometimes slightly damaged, into old age. However, behind that usually unremarkable face may be an individual who can turn his hand to surgery or satellite communications, drive just about any vehicle on or off the road, identify a dozen or so edible mushrooms and plants, swim most rivers fully clothed, or order a meal in fluent Malay, Russian, German or Arabic.

There is of course one other talent that all SAS men, serving or retired, have in common. They have all been taught by experts to dispatch an enemy with cool efficiency, either with modern weapons, or with improvised ones, or with their bare hands. 'Where else,' said one veteran, 'would you meet a man who has spent twenty-two years employed by Her Majesty the Queen to kill people?' This book is dedicated to them, they know who they are, though their neighbours may not, the ones who decided out of loyalty to the Regiment not to write a book or make a film themselves.

ONE

—

THE ORIGINALS

When SAS troopers are dispatched to a remote corner of the world on a top secret mission today, they use weapons and equipment that might astonish their predecessors, but the daily hardships they face and the basic tactics they use have hardly changed at all since their regiment was born. As recent history has shown, the life-threatening situations that Britain's elite troops have a habit of getting themselves into are rarely resolved by modern technology or some twenty-first century wonder-gun. In the final analysis it is the individual, alone or with a small, closely knit team, using his brain as much as brawn, who finds a way out and lives to fight another day.

So what is it that sets these men apart from the rest of today's modern military forces and turns them, in the eyes of the public, into real-life versions of Arnold Schwarzenegger, forever dodging bullets and stitching gaping wounds with the suture kit hidden in the handle of their razor-sharp Rambo knives? The reality, as any new SAS man will tell you, is rather different. First comes the sudden realization that the odds of you being killed or maimed early on in your special forces career are pretty high, and that you may soon be risking your life in places that most normal people would avoid like the plague. Very few people in war meet a 'clean death' with a bullet placed neatly between the eyes, dead before they hit the ground. There is almost always the blood and the suffering before the morphine arrives, if it arrives at all. Then there is the strict rule which forbids talking about where you have been and what you have done, unless of course you leave the army and become a wealthy author, as the odd veteran has done in recent times. Wherever there are dangerous and difficult confrontations, the SAS will be ready to move. So why do so many young soldiers dream of joining the SAS? Is it for the mystique of belonging to the best team, the 'first eleven' of their nation's elite forces, or could it be simple machismo, being able to take on the toughest bar-room fighters with their bare hands?

To find the answer, which is neither of the above as mature SAS men do not need to prove anything to anyone, the reader is obliged to look back in time to the man who generated the idea of using small commando-style teams behind the enemy's lines. The concept, it must be said, was not quite so original as some would have you believe. The notion of creeping up on the enemy and carrying out all kinds of mischief behind his back was nothing new even in the days of the ancient Huns or the barbarians. What made David Stirling different was, initially, the rather gentlemanly way he chose to fight his country's enemies. Later on he would discover that in all-out warfare there is neither the time nor the opportunity to play by the rules, and that, if for one moment you drop your guard, the result can be, and usually is, fatal.

For the uninitiated it was quite easy to misinterpret Stirling's character, and in the post-war years more than one not especially left-wing radical called him a fascist or accused him and his ideas of being neo-colonialist. Nothing could have been further from the truth. He was a firm believer in the right of the individual to choose his own destiny, and could dispatch most critics, not with a stiletto dagger, but with his quick wit. Even in old age, the sparkle in his youthful eye could bring a smile to many of the world's leaders like Margaret Thatcher and Ronald Reagan.

More than anything, ordinary soldiers liked and respected him, which is a rare achievement for most 'Ruperts' (officers). When he was recovering in hospital from an illness shortly before his death, in 1990, some of Stirling's friends, all serving or retired SAS men, called in to see him. His room, near the top of the building, was full of get-well cards and flowers from well-wishers. When the last of the visitors had finally left, Stirling opened a large package, a present from some of the men. Inside was enough climbing rope to reach all the way from his window to the pavement below. An attached note suggested that 'if he didn't think it worth his while escaping, he could always hang himself'.

Stirling was born in Scotland in 1915, the son of Brigadier-General Archibald Stirling of Keir. His father had been gassed in the trenches by the Germans, so consequently the raising of the young David was left very much to his mother, the Hon. Margaret, née Fraser, a daughter of Lord Lovat. Despite a strict upbringing, his childhood was a happy one.

There were no beatings or punishments but a strict code of discipline reigned. At an early age Stirling was taught not to cry in the face of pain or adversity. When he was eight he was bitten on the leg by an adder while roaming in the heather on the island of Mull. For a while it seemed likely that he would lose the leg, but his mother and the local doctor nursed him patiently back to health and the leg was saved. This was not the first time he had known suffering. As a small child it was noticed that he had a speech impediment and doctors had operated on his tongue. Later, in his teens, he contracted typhoid and it was only with luck – or perhaps it was destiny – that he survived to reach manhood. Religion played a serious part in his upbringing, his parents being practising Roman Catholics, and in the same year as the adder incident he was sent to the Catholic college of Ampleforth with his three brothers: Bill, who was later to serve with him in the SAS, Peter and Hugh. Closest to David was his sister Margaret. He had another sister, Irene, making six children in all.

At school he met Freddy de Guingand in the Officer Training Corps, and Guingand was to prove a valuable friend in Stirling's later years. He was to become General Sir Bernard (later Field Marshal Viscount) Montgomery's Chief of Staff during the Second World War. Whether David Stirling had military ambitions in his childhood is unclear, but it is evident that, in his youth, wild open spaces enchanted him. By the time he was a young man, hillwalking, shooting, deerstalking and mountaineering were skills he had acquired with a certain flair, and it is said that he was capable of stalking a deer and killing it with his bare hands. Brother Bill was a skilled rabbit poacher in his youth, and Stirling and his brothers took part in many of these adventures together.

On the academic front Stirling's interests lay with the arts rather than the sciences. Due to his ill health in childhood there were a succession of tutors to concentrate his mind and educate him, and he eventually went to Trinity College, Cambridge, where he read architecture. By then he had grown to an impressive six feet five inches. Politically he was known to have contempt for the Communist clique whom he looked upon as misguided and unable to recognize the main failing of that concept, its totalitarianism. Not for Stirling the long political debates into the early hours. He was much happier painting the town red. He became known as a 'bit of a lad' with his fellow students and clearly enjoyed having fun.

As a reasonably talented artist he left university and went to France in the 1930s, where he sampled the delights of Parisian life. Montmartre and the Rive Gauche became his haunts, and it was here that he encountered for the first time in his life a truly cosmopolitan society. However, his artistic career never really got off the ground. It was perhaps due to the distractions of horse-racing and gambling, as well as a certain penchant for good-looking girls, and Paris was certainly ideal for all of these in the 1930s. When boredom eventually set in, he then decided to climb Mount Everest; 1937 and 1938 found him in the Swiss Alps and the Rocky Mountains, training for an adventure he would never undertake.

On hearing that war had been declared, during an expedition on horseback along the banks of the Rio Grande in 1939, Stirling lost no time in returning home where he enlisted in the Scots Guards, joining his brothers Hugh and William. At the age of twenty-four he was posted to the Guards Depot at Pirbright Barracks, and it soon became apparent to the young soldier that 'senseless marching up and down' was not for him.

But instead of becoming bored and frustrated by the enforced discipline of this period of his life, he rather laughed at it, and in particular he laughed at the drill sergeants. A short journey by train took Stirling to London and the bright lights of the West End. As often as possible he would escape from the camp and enjoy himself.

13

Recruits at Pirbright were forbidden such night-time activities but Stirling soon discovered that the perimeter fences were a minor obstacle to his social life and he scaled them frequently for visits to White's Club in the West End of London, for sessions at the gambling tables. William, Viscount Whitelaw, who was at Pirbright at the same time as Stirling, spoke of him as 'quite irresponsible', and he recalls the time when Stirling was detailed to instruct him on the duties of the orderly officer. Stirling simply ignored the subject and went off to London for a night out. Described as 'an irresponsible and unremarkable soldier' at the end of his training, Stirling was posted to the 5th Battalion of the Scots Guards who were training at this time as ski troops.

Being one of the rare recruits who had already learned to ski, and with a good practical knowledge of mountains, he was almost immediately promoted to sergeant. The Scots Guards were training for deployment to Finland, but by the time they were ready to move Finland had fallen to the German advance, and Britain's Expeditionary Force in support of the Finns never materialized. Back at Pirbright, Stirling controlled his boredom by more visits to White's Club and to the London nightspots, and it was during one of these night-time drinking sessions that he first heard of Robert Laycock's project to create a unit of commandos from the ranks of the Brigade of Guards. Stirling's taste for adventure was aroused and he applied to join. His application was accepted and as a newly commissioned second lieutenant he was soon undergoing commando training in Scotland where, of course, he felt perfectly at home.

Another recruit to the new unit was Randolph Churchill who also had joined the commandos through his connections at White's Club, and their mutual interest in games of chance and backgammon brought them into frequent contact.

In February 1941, as a fully fledged member of 8 Commando, Stirling sailed to the Middle East as a member of 'Layforce', Robert Laycock's newborn unit, via Cape Town. In June of the previous year, British airborne forces had been born. Russian troops had experimented with airborne training before the war, and Germany already had one parachute division, Fliegerdivision 7, which had been deployed during the invasions of Holland and Belgium in May 1940. It was in response to these actions that the British Army created its first parachute-trained force, the 11th Special Air Service Battalion consisting of 500 volunteers. In 1941 this group was renamed the First Parachute Battalion.

Having seen South Africa briefly on his journey, Stirling vowed some day to return to see more of that country with its 'magnificent scenery and wildlife'.[1] In March 1941 Layforce was in Suez training for a planned attack on the island of Rhodes, but with the Germans' skilful airborne assault of Crete the plans were quickly changed.

Stirling's unit moved westwards to Mersa Matruh from where 8 Commando carried out night raids against enemy coastal positions at Gazala and at the aerodrome at Bomba. Each of the raids involved an approach by gunboats or larger craft, but they all failed due to bad weather or because the ships were spotted by enemy aircraft and bombed. Stirling's first taste of military action ended in failure.

Shortly afterwards Layforce was disbanded and Stirling, once again, became inactive and extremely bored. Peter, his brother, was serving at the British Embassy in Cairo and had an apartment in the plush Garden City

[1] After the war Stirling created the Capricorn African Society (CAS).

15

area. Stirling took full advantage of this, continuing his social life in Egypt as he had done in London. Despite the disapproval of senior officers he would abscond from camp for these night-time excursions and frequently be absent when he should have been on parade in the morning. His military career risked coming to an abrupt end when, during a night exercise, he walked into a thorn branch and seriously injured an eye. Another version of the story suggested he had in fact tripped over a tent guy-rope in a drunken stupor, but whatever the cause of this injury he found himself being branded as a malingerer, facing a probable charge of cowardice, and an inevitable court martial. However, on returning from hospital where his eye wound had been stitched, he encountered Captain Jock Lewes in the officers' mess. Stirling knew Lewes already, and liked this quiet and rather aloof Welsh Guardsman. Lewes, who had been a rowing blue at Oxford, was exceptionally fit, and told David Stirling he had managed to obtain fifty parachutes and was hoping to try them out. In fact the parachutes had been destined for India, but as most serving and ex-members of the SAS will tell you, good 'kit' often goes astray. Lewes had been given permission by Robert Laycock to conduct experiments in parachuting, and this project instantly appealed to Stirling. Together they embarked on what was to prove to be an incredible and dangerous adventure.

With Lewes and two other volunteers, Stirling made his first parachute jump from a Vickers Valentia aircraft in the spring of 1941, the men attaching the static lines of their parachutes to the passenger seat legs which seemed fairly solidly fixed. Diving out of the Valentia, Stirling's parachute caught the tailplane and a panel of the canopy ripped. With his parachute flapping wildly and out of control, his descent was, to say the least, rapid. With a tremendous impact Stirling hit the ground, seriously injuring his back. He was again rushed to hospital in Cairo where for a while he thought he might never walk again. However, after about a week, he was moving around on crutches and it was during this enforced period of recovery that he conceived the idea for a small, highly trained and motivated military unit that could work deep behind the enemy lines.

It might well have been his childhood experiences in the Scottish Highlands that sparked the idea. Every deerstalker knows what happens when a large group of hunters and beaters march across the hills in search of game. Your prey immediately takes off and runs for cover. The British Army, as far as Stirling could see, was still using the same tactics it had employed in the First World War, with set-piece battles taking place after heavy artillery bombardments to soften the enemy's defences. Only then would tanks and infantry advance, and losses of men and equipment were enormous.

What was needed to defeat the modern enemy, Stirling argued, was stealth and cunning. With Jock Lewes, he began formulating a plan for the creation of a small commando unit and Stirling carefully worded a handwritten letter to General Sir Claude Auchinleck, Commander-in-Chief of Middle East Forces. In this letter Stirling proposed the creation of a 'Special Unit Service' operating by land, sea and air and comprising teams of twelve men in three groups of four.[2] The commando units would be parachuted behind enemy lines at night twelve miles from their objectives, hide and observe their targets the next day, and then carry out their raids under cover of darkness. He proposed that each team would carry around sixty explosive and incendiary bombs and

[2] This was the origin of the four-man section or 'brick' which is standard in today's British army.

small arms and, on completion of their tasks, exfiltrate into the desert on foot. The Long Range Desert Group, Stirling suggested, would be ideal for picking them up later at prearranged rendezvous points. His first targets would be the enemy airfields of Gazala and Tmimi.

Stirling took a taxi to Middle East Command Head-quarters and walking with the aid of his crutches attempted to gain entry. But the sentry on the gate demanded to see his pass and when the young Lieu-tenant Stirling apologized and said he seemed to have arrived without it, the sentry turned him away. Pausing for thought, Stirling noticed a gap in the wire fence and when the sentry's back was turned, he slipped inside. Within seconds he was spotted by the sentry who began shouting 'Stop that man!' but by then Stirling had aban-doned his crutches and was hobbling up the stairs inside the building. Crashing into an office marked 'Adjutant General' he came face to face with a major he had hoped never to see again. It was his instructor from his training days at Pirbright. The conversation was short and unpleasant and the major ordered him out of the office immediately. With the continuing shouts from the sentry in the background, Stirling tried another door.

Now his luck changed, for behind the door was the Deputy Chief of the General Staff, Lieutenant-General Neil Ritchie, a large, agreeable man, popular with his troops. 'Sir,' proclaimed the young subaltern, his legs only just holding him, 'I am Lieutenant Stirling, Scots Guards.' He apologized for having burst in and explained to Ritchie that he had a matter of great urgency to bring to his attention. With that he offered his handwritten proposals to the general, and Ritchie read them carefully, twice. By the time his old training major tracked him down, Stirling was sitting comfort-ably in an armchair.

Three days later he was called back to see General Auchinleck. After much debate and carefully defending his ideas for the formation of a new unit Stirling was given instructions to recruit six officers and sixty men. Brigadier Dudley Clarke, who was in charge of deception operations in the Middle East theatre of war, suggested the title for his unit, the Special Air Service Brigade, L Detachment.

Given the rank of captain, he set about selecting his officers and men. His first and most obvious choice was Jock Lewes who had distinguished himself in action already in the war, and Stirling wasted no time in contacting him. The others would be the best of his colleagues from Layforce and the Scots Guards. His task was hindered by bureaucrats within the army who clearly resented the unorthodox behaviour of the young upstart Stirling. The newly appointed commander of L Detachment SAS wasted no time in referring to his superior-officer critics as 'layer upon layer of fossilized shit', and the men under his new command chuckled in agreement.

After a good deal of gentle persuasion, for he was unconvinced initially of Stirling's plans, Jock Lewes agreed to join, and with him he brought Sergeants Jim Almonds and Pat Riley and Privates Jim Blakeney and Ernest Lilley. Ernie Bond, Stirling's platoon sergeant, volunteered immediately. Others included Bob Bennett, Johnny Cooper, Reg Seekings, Dave Kershaw and Bob Tate, who made up the group known affectionately in today's SAS circles as 'the Originals'. Their base was to be at Kabrit, halfway between Cairo and Port Said on the banks of the Great Bitter Lake. With the addition of Blair 'Paddy' Mayne, a rugby-playing Ulsterman whom Stirling recruited in a prison cell where Mayne was facing a probable court martial for punching his commanding officer, and four other officers, L Detachment of the Special Air Service was born.

There are many common misconceptions about the desert, and David Stirling's newly formed unit had much to learn just to stay alive in this very hostile environment. Firstly, the area of operations of the SAS during the campaign in the Western Desert was not some romantic Lawrence of Arabia landscape of rolling sand dunes. About 80 per cent of the region is made up of rock formations. During winter and spring the contrast in temperatures can be immense, and one can often awake to find the ground, and oneself, frozen. A shortage of natural protective features allows little shelter from howling winds that burn the skin and eyes; and sandstorms or the more frightening khamsins, fierce southern winds that throw up a wall of sand and dust several hundreds of feet high as they advance, are positive nightmares.

One solution proposed by the planners was the use of gas masks to combat the effects of these storms but, as was so often the case, such ideas were divorced from reality – wearing a gas mask in a sandstorm, the SAS soon discovered, was completely impracticable. Each morning the men would start the day wearing their thick battledress tunics and trousers, army greatcoats, boots and blankets, and these would be gradually shed as the heat of the morning increased. By midday they would be clad in nothing but boots or sandals, shorts or trousers and some form of head covering against the relentless heat and glare of the sun.

Temperatures at the height of the summer would frequently reach 120 degrees Fahrenheit, and at sunset, when the desert chills suddenly, they would reverse the procedure, climbing back into their warm clothes. The detachment's modern-day counterparts would learn of these hazards themselves nearly fifty years later during the Gulf War.

Then there were the flies. Wherever men lived in the desert the flies would live too, and stopping for a moment in an oasis or trying to cook a meal would be an invitation to swarms of the creatures. Mosquitoes on the other hand were fairly rare, and would normally only be found close to desert wells, pools or in cultivated areas. There were scorpions, the yellow ones being more plentiful than the black species, praying mantises, desert foxes, and snakes. Few of the men with their roots in urban or rural Britain knew anything of the exotic and diverse species of reptiles and 'creepie-crawlies' that abounded in these lands, but they quickly learned the difference between the horn-nosed viper and other less dangerous species that might slither or crawl into their sleeping quarters at night.

Stirling began training his men to operate in the desert environment, but most of what he taught was based on trial and error for, like the men under his command, his knowledge of the desert was minimal. Many years later, when asked about the original idea for the SAS, he was quick to point out that he was not the sole creator. In 1984 at the opening ceremony of the new Stirling Lines SAS base in Hereford, he expressed his personal gratitude to the 'co-founders', the original 'Dirty Dozen' officers and men who were with him at the beginning.

Captain Jock Lewes became the key to the training programme. Lewes set himself the task of testing, firstly, himself, and later the men, so as to be able to fight and survive in this hostile environment. He would set out at night carrying a bergen and walk on a compass bearing, reach what he considered to be a safe halfway mark, and walk back again. Gradually Lewes increased the weight of the bergen and the distance covered until he was near total exhaustion. In this way, the famous SAS marches were born. Never leaving word of his route at base, he could easily have perished in the barren wastes of the desert, but this was part of Lewes's psychology. If he knew that he could be rescued in the event of accident or exhaustion, he would not have been in a real life-threatening situation, and he had to make the training programme as realistic as possible.

As he marched he would keep note of the distance covered by counting stones or pebbles, transferring each of them from one trouser pocket to the other after a hundred paces. Using this simple but rather inaccurate technique, he was able to make a rough estimate of the distance he had covered. He estimated each stride as thirty inches, and each pebble represented eighty-three yards. Ten pebbles equalled eight hundred and thirty yards, and there were approximately twenty-one pebbles to a mile.

Lewes also researched the effects of water denial, and discovered that with training his consumption could be greatly reduced. On one occasion, following a twenty-mile route march through the desert in daytime with the men, he checked their water bottles. He was pleasantly surprised to find that nobody had completely emptied his canteen. When challenged by a soldier to show his own consumption, the men were amazed to discover that Lewes had not touched a drop. The Welsh Guards captain, instantly and without reservation, had won the respect of his men.

As will be seen later in the chapter on selection (Chapter Two), this relationship between officers and other ranks in the SAS continues today, and the acceptance of an officer by the men he commands is probably more pronounced in the SAS Regiment than in any other of the British Army.

Jock Lewes devised a rigorous training programme at Kabrit which encompassed parachute and fitness training, weapons familiarization and marksmanship. Recruits were encouraged to learn as much as possible about the enemy's weapons and tactics, and, inevitably, how to deal quietly and efficiently with an enemy sentry at night. He and Stirling were convinced that the Russian soldiers' saying, 'train hard, fight easy', was the solution to most of their problems, and the other aspects of the job which included complex logistics would be resolved with careful planning.

Lewes took his work very seriously and would often be seen in his tent late at night working away at his plans by the light of a hurricane lamp. The result of one of his late-night projects was the invention of the Lewes bomb, a small portable plastic explosive device that could be placed on to an enemy aircraft or other target. The resulting explosion would create a fire, ideal for commando operations and for causing maximum damage with minimum size and weight. The fuses for these bombs were time pencils which consisted of a glass tube containing acid. When broken, the acid would burn through a metal wire releasing a coiled spring which ignited the explosive charge after a delay of either fifteen or thirty minutes. Despite a certain unreliability with the timing system – they sometimes went off sooner or later than expected – the Lewes bomb became a valuable new weapon of war.

Ever short of kit and stores the men of L Detachment SAS 'borrowed' most of the items they needed from wherever they could acquire them, and soon the camp boasted a piano and many other comforts of home. To call them thieves and scroungers would be an insult.

Suffice to say, they were extremely adept at obtaining the seemingly impossible. In the many military camps that littered the desert at this time there was little secrecy as we know it today, and on one occasion Stirling's men were driving along a winding track towards the coast when they found themselves crossing an American landing ground. Aircraft were dispersed all around them and one of the SAS soldiers remarked how easy it would be to drop a few Lewes bombs into their cockpits as they passed. Nobody had challenged them, they were a ragged and unshaven lot, and it became obvious to the men that if the Germans' or the Italians' defences were as weak as the Americans', the amount of havoc they could cause would be incredible. David Stirling's mind was working overtime thinking of all the dastardly possibilities available for future operations. If you dared to do it, you would probably succeed, at least for a while. And what if you drove a captured German vehicle behind their lines? Would anyone pay any attention to you?

L Detachment, with its seven officers and sixty men, had been given six months at Kabrit to prepare for combat and in August 1941 the major priority was for parachute training. Stirling, with the help of 216 Squadron RAF, acquired the services of a Bristol Bombay transport aircraft, and a static-line rail was rigged up inside the fuselage. When the time came, the novice parachutists of the first stick jumped for the first time. All went well and without serious incident, although some of the landings were a little hard. The second group prepared to jump but then disaster struck. On the next flight the second stick began to exit the Bombay and to Stirling's horror their chutes failed to deploy. The RAF dispatcher noticed that the clips used to attach the parachutes' static lines to the rail were unfastening as the men jumped and he grabbed the parachutist who was poised in the door and held him. But two of the men had already plunged to their deaths. Stirling immediately abandoned the training programme for the day and called his men around him. He issued them with hundreds of cigarettes to calm their nerves and promised that the clips would be changed, the problem resolved, and that on the next flight he would be the first to jump. The next day he was indeed the first parachutist out of the Bombay and the training programme continued without further incident.

The new unit now needed a proper identity and Corporal Duncan Tait came up with the design for a cap badge. Often described as the 'Winged Dagger',[3] the badge is in fact a flaming sword. The light blue wings and the dark-blue shield represent the colours of Oxford and Cambridge University boat crews in which several SAS members had served. The motto 'Who Dares Wins' is inscribed across the blade of the sword.

The badge was worn on a variety of headdresses at its inception, then a completely impractical white beret was chosen. As the men discovered, wearing a white beret in the streets of Cairo was asking for trouble and many jokes were made at their expense. SAS men responded frequently with their fists. Fortunately, for 'operational reasons' the white beret did not last long, and was soon changed to a sand-coloured one. Jock Lewes designed the shoulder wings, the top row of feathers are dark blue, the lower ones are light blue. A white parachute with five rigging lines is in the centre.

On 17 November 1941, L Detachment carried out its first operations. The plan originally proposed by Stirling to Auchinleck was to attack the enemy's landing

[3] Many, including David Stirling, referred to the 'Winged Dagger' as King Arthur's sword, but the SAS Regimental Association in 1996 finally confirmed it as the sword of Damocles.

grounds at Tmimi and Gazala, the raiders would parachute into the desert at night, advance to their targets, lay up during the daytime and attack the following night. It was to be a near total disaster.

On the night of 16 November 1941, five Bristol Bombays from 216 Squadron, carrying Stirling's paratroopers, crossed the Allied lines and headed out over the Mediterranean. The weather on take-off was clear, but during the two-hour flight the aircraft flew into a violent storm. Unable to establish their exact position owing to poor visibility and then anti-aircraft fire which claimed several direct hits, the mission was aborted, but not before several of the paratroopers had jumped. Stirling parachuted with the men from his aircraft over what they hoped would be the planned landing zone, and was knocked out when he hit the ground.

There was a violent sandstorm blowing and, after regaining consciousness, it took Stirling hours to regroup his troops. Some of his men were injured and many were missing. Discovering that the man carrying the detonators for the Lewes bombs had vanished, Stirling realized that to go on would be pointless. The survivors made their way on foot to the coast and finally arrived at their prearranged rendezvous point with the Long Range Desert Group after a march of more than fifty miles behind enemy lines. Two-thirds of Stirling's first raiding force were either killed, captured or wounded. Of the entire group only four officers and eighteen other ranks returned to Kabrit. Including their commanding officer, there were twenty-two survivors. That number was to become significant in later years. The Regular Army regiment of the SAS today is 22 Regiment, and David Stirling's offices up until his death in November 1990 were at 22 South Audley Street in London.

Surprisingly, critics of this small commando force failed to call for its disbandment following the disastrous first operation and, undeterred, Stirling persisted in spite of his critics at Middle East Headquarters. In December 1941 the remnants of L Detachment carried out raids on eight enemy airfields. This time the Long Range Desert Group delivered the commando teams to start points in occupied territory from where the attacks were launched. In this operation more than ninety enemy aircraft were destroyed. Returning to Kabrit, Jock Lewes's patrol was attacked by a Messerschmitt 110 and Lewes received a terrible leg wound. He died before the unit reached their base. In regimental parlance, he failed to 'beat the clock', an expression which has become the in-house description of any SAS man who dies on a mission.

The SAS's adopted poem, taken from the verse play *Hassan* written at the turn of the century by James Elroy Flecker, symbolizes the Regiment's philosophy of its operations. Hassan, master of the caravan, on seeing strangers, says:

> 'But who are ye in rags and rotten shoes
> You dirty bearded blocking the way?'
> 'We are the pilgrims, master
> We shall go always a little further
> It may be beyond that last blue mountain
>   barr'd with snow
> Across that angry or that glimmering sea.'

The poem is inscribed on the clock tower at SAS Headquarters in Hereford on which the names of men killed in action are listed.

It is not intended here to catalogue the individual acts of bravery carried out by members of the SAS during the Second World War nor to document all of their raids, as almost each operation is worthy of a volume in its own right. Missions carried out by Stirling's men became more and more daring, and with cunning and ingenuity hit the enemy hundreds of miles behind their lines. Following these successful raids in the North African theatre, the Regiment established a foothold in British military history that lives on today in legend. The very mention of the SAS brings to mind visions of men cloaked in black, faces hidden, and guns drawn. Critics have often questioned the value of small, elite forces and their overall worth to military campaigns, but the demoralizing effect on the enemy's troops of being attacked from the rear when least expected is psychologically highly effective. Today's terrorists have in some respects used to their own advantage the techniques of speed, aggression and surprise that were developed to perfection in those early years by the SAS.

Stirling had without realizing it changed the face of modern warfare and brought the use of stealth and surprise into the modern soldier's training manual. In the months that followed Jock Lewes's death, L Detachment SAS led by Stirling and Paddy Mayne continued to carry out many daring raids on German and Italian airfields and other targets of opportunity along the way, and with the close co-operation of the Long Range Desert Group and the adoption of the Willys jeep, it looked at the time as if nothing could stop them. Twin Vickers 'K' machine guns were fitted to the jeeps, and soon the SAS was carrying out hit-and-run raids on enemy airfields, driving under the cover of darkness down the runways with all guns blazing and planting Lewes bombs on enemy aircraft. The effect was tremendous and terrifying. General Rommel, the enemy commander in North Africa, would later admit that the SAS had done more damage to the German forces than any other unit of its size in the Second World War.

British soldiers were not the only ones wreaking havoc behind enemy lines. Stirling's soldiers fought alongside Free French troops whom he had managed to recruit in Alexandria. Negotiating with their commander, who refused to let his men fight under an Englishman, Stirling replied, 'I am not English, I am a Scot. What about our old alliance?'[4] He got his men.

By 1943 a second regiment of the SAS had been created, and the command went to Stirling's brother Bill. The Free French formed their own SAS Regiment and they, and the Greek Sacred Squadron, were put under David Stirling's command. And then the inevitable happened. Stirling, while lying up after recceing an enemy aerodrome at night, was spotted by a young Arab. Appearing friendly, the Arab boy offered him food and water, but led Stirling straight to an Italian patrol. Before he could do anything the Arab pulled out a pistol and pushed it into Stirling's ribs. Furious at having been tricked this way, he suddenly grabbed the boy by the legs and spun him around his head, but the Italians closed in on him and he found himself a prisoner.

Despite numerous attempts to escape during the rest of the war years, David Stirling's fighting days were over. With their commanding officer captured, the remaining officers and men needed a new leader, and one was waiting in the wings who fitted the role perfectly – Paddy Mayne.

In the years that followed, Mayne led the Regiment with skill and tremendous personal courage. Disliked by many of the staff officers at headquarters for his total disregard for conformity, Mayne, more perhaps than any other member of the SAS, epitomized the symbol of

[4] Referring to Scotland's ancient friendship with the French.

what an SAS soldier should be: solid, courageous, and full of surprises. Unlike David Stirling, Paddy Mayne was very much a loner, and apart from his occasional violent outbursts he was greatly respected and feared by the men who served under him. With Bill Stirling commanding the 2nd SAS Regiment, Mayne led the 1st SAS through the desert war, and then into Europe, perfecting the skills that Stirling had developed. Most of the veterans of the war who served near or alongside Mayne are of the opinion that he should have won the Victoria Cross at least once. Unfortunately a superior officer needs to recommend this award, and there was rarely an officer as far forward in the line of battle as Paddy Mayne.

Blair 'Paddy' Mayne died in a car crash in Newtownards, Northern Ireland, on 15 December 1955.

TWO

SELECTION

The principles for selecting SAS soldiers laid down more than fifty years ago by Stirling, Lewes and Mayne in the Western Desert remain today. However, the role envisaged for the Regiment by its founders has altered greatly, and critics, including some old warriors who recall distant campaigns of the past, might be slightly perplexed by the modern selection course and the continuation training which follows it. An ex-trooper who served in 22 SAS in Oman, the Falklands, Northern Ireland and other lesser known conflicts remembers the long and exhausting process that finally resulted in being 'badged' into the Regiment:

> You've geared yourself up for it, trained like an athlete and you know it is going to be hard, but there's that unknown element that creeps in. Will they push you too far, beyond your limits? People actually die out there on the hills trying to reach those RVs [rendezvous] in time, not often perhaps, but the fear is there whatever anyone tells you. At the end of the day you're on your own and that's when you really find out about yourself. You're tabbing [the Paras' word for a brisk walk, the equivalent of the Royal Marines' 'yomping'] along making good time, and then this wave of panic comes

over you suddenly. Are you on the right route? If you're not, and the DS [Directing Staff] don't find you, you'll end up exhausted and unconscious with the crows of Brecon feasting on your eyeballs. When you're out there on the Beacons in the middle of the night in a hailstorm, you make sure your navigation is spot on and you'd better not make any mistakes. Then, if you're lucky, you find the RV, and that's when your confidence comes back. The fitness thing is very important, it's true, but you've got to study the map, read it like a book until the contours come alive. It's really a matter of confidence-building. Some of the country boys who have grown up in the wild take to it like a duck to water, but it's harder for a city kid.

That ex-member of 22 SAS still walks in the Brecon Beacons but today, in retirement, he walks with his family and their dog, and solely for pleasure. Occasionally, though, he will put on his battered bergen, and alone, or with another retired SAS man, he will do a trek. Sometimes, when an old comrade dies, his closest friends will 'do a walk' in his memory. This is traditionally followed by a large consumption of alcohol in a local pub. SAS men rarely show their emotions in public, but years of service in one of the most dangerous professions in the world leave hard memories.

Selection is divided into phases, and the hopeful recruit must convince the SAS Directing Staff that he has the required physical and mental stamina to complete it. It lasts three weeks and culminates in the endurance march, known to those who attempt it as the 'Long Drag'. Run twice-yearly, the courses take place in winter and summer months, and a candidate may experience both seasons in the hills if he fails to pass first time.

Candidates for selection training come not only from the Army, but also from the other armed services and must be aged between nineteen and thirty-four. An officer cannot apply until he is twenty-two. Any man serving in the British Army, Royal Air Force or Royal Navy can apply as long as he has at least three years left to serve. Members of the Territorial Army's 21st or 23rd Regiments SAS can also apply to join 22 (pronounced 'two-two'). If a man is accepted, after much form-filling he is taken with other hopefuls to SAS headquarters in Hereford where it is explained to him what he is letting himself in for. The usual routine is to welcome the candidate and to advise him not to get too comfortable as he won't be staying for long. From the first day his reaction to events and his attitude are painstakingly noted. The spotlight is on him and in all probability he will fail. This simple fact, made clear to him at the very start, is enough to discourage many who try.

Run by the Regiment's Training Wing, the selection process begins with the standard army battle fitness test. Assuming that he passes this, and he should do to be in the army, navy or air force, though some do not, he will then move on to three weeks of progressively punishing marches over the Welsh hills carrying an increasingly heavy load. To begin with, he will walk in a group and his bergen will weigh just 11 kilos.

Gradually the marches increase in distance and he will practise his day and night navigation, all the time being closely observed by the Training Wing staff. After several group marches the men walk in pairs, and then finally alone. Now the weight of his bergen is increased to 30 kilos and the candidate is expected to complete the routes on time and without complaint. The men running the course, some of the toughest of the Regiment's senior NCOs, will all the time be looking for physical or mental weaknesses in the candidates and will already have identified potential successes and failures in the ranks. Although frowned upon by some of their superiors, bets are sometimes made on the candidates by the Training Wing sergeants. There is no quota to be filled and they are not under any obligation to pass a percentage of candidates. As the days pass the numbers diminish. The final Long Drag route that prospective SAS men must follow consists of an 80-kilometre trek in the Welsh hills. This distance must be covered in twenty hours using map and compass, and the only way to arrive at the RVs in time is to run much of the way. An average speed over the ground of 4 kilometres per hour is required. By comparison the Parachute Regiment's P Company endurance march covers 28 kilometres in 4 hours carrying a bergen weighing 22 kilos with a half-hour break for rest; an average speed of 7 kilometres per hour. A quick glance at the above figures might suggest that any paratrooper could probably complete the SAS course. Although the bergen weight has increased by 8 kilos he should be capable of completing the route in around 11 or 12 hours.

However, the fatigue encountered after fast walking and running across the Brecon Beacons where boots slip on the grass tussocks and you can easily break an ankle in the dark demands incredible stamina and stubborn, if not fanatical, dedication. One recruit remembered climbing to the top of Fan Fawr in shirt and trousers during summer selection:

The sweat is pouring off you and the straps of your bergen are rubbing away the skin on your shoulders even though you've padded them with foam and tape, and you've been tabbing for hours. I kept going over the summit, running down the other side and the heavens opened suddenly. Within seconds I was drenched so I stopped and put on a sweater and my windproof. You're freezing cold by then. Minutes later, crossing the stream, the sun comes out. Now you're sweating again. In the end you just hack it wearing as little as possible, try to keep your body core temperature normal and resist the elements by willpower. It is not so bad when the weather stays constant, but that's rare in those hills. Sometimes the winds gust at 50 miles an hour and you're on your hands and knees crawling on to the ridge. When the cloud comes down or at night you could easily walk into space and fall 100 feet or more. Above all you've got to keep a sense of humour, have the staying power to succeed, and simply not give in.

During summer selection the candidate must contend with heat, horseflies and occasional downpours, and in winter he may encounter ice, snow and blizzards where navigation becomes extremely difficult. Trying to take a bearing on a patch of white hillside is testing for even the most experienced hillwalkers. One badged member of 22 SAS advised trainees to avoid taking compass bearings on local sheep which can prove attractive landmarks. 'Problem is they move when you least expect it!'

Even at the height of summer the summit of Corn Du or Pen-Y-Fan may be lost in cloud and lashed with hailstones. Keeping a close check on one's exact position on the map at all times is the key to success. At RV points along his way the candidate may be asked to accomplish a task such as stripping a weapon (it may be foreign) or emptying his bergen and carrying its contents in a poncho to the next RV. He may also be encouraged to 'take the weight off his feet' and have a cup of coffee from the sergeant's Thermos. Any candidate would be well advised to decline such kind offers if he hopes to succeed.

Some years ago the bergens were filled with numbered bricks to make up the weight (in those days 55 pounds) but now each candidate is encouraged to carry more useful items of kit. As well as the bergen he must also wear standard issue PLCE (personal load-carriage equipment) webbing and carry his rifle, normally the SA-80 individual weapon – which is disliked and rarely used by members of the SAS – without a sling as though patrolling during an operation. Aspiring SAS men will often rehearse the selection course in their parent units and by training in their spare time. One who passed remembers travelling down to the Brecon Beacons at weekends and marching alone for months in order to acquire the level of fitness the SAS demands. On his first attempt he was told to 'Go home and brush up your navigation.' The following year, feeling at home in the hills, he passed selection and was badged.

A standard swimming test is included in the selection process beginning with a short swim around a very cold and deep pool. Before completing selection the candidate will have to face a 1,000-metre swim in combat clothing.

Included in this stage is a gruelling crawl through a series of muddy tunnels which lead into a stagnant pool. Any candidate who suffers from claustrophobia or the terror of drowning is well advised to give up now, or else confront and beat such fears. Entry to the tunnels is through an iron drain cover which is ceremoniously slammed after you enter. Finding yourself in the dark, you then climb down a ladder. At the bottom, inside the tunnel, the task is to find your way out through a warren of routes leading to one of a number of exits and if you are fortunate, you won't end up in the stagnant pool.

Candidates who give up at any point of selection have very little chance of ever joining 22 SAS. 'It's one thing to reach the end and get turned down,' says an ex-member, 'you can always have a second go and with luck they (Training Wing) will admire your bottle and pass you. But once you throw your hand in that's you gone for ever.'

A commando assault course is included in the tests with the candidates allowed very little sleep between activities. Everything is done with a view to pushing them to their physical and mental limits with minor punishments such as press-ups for failing to abide by the rules or general sloppiness in the training area. Observers suggest that there is very little difference between ordinary commando training such as that carried out by other elite units of the world's armies, and SAS selection. In essence this argument holds some truth but perhaps the difference lies in the time-scale and the failure rate. No other unit crams so much physical strain and a demand for excellence into such a short time-scale as the SAS, and on successful completion of selection there is no guarantee that the exhausted soldier will be accepted by the officers and non-commissioned officers. In brief, 'If they don't like you and the way you behave, you won't get in,' says one ex-NCO. The tasks become harder each day. 'You might suddenly find you're being told to pull an artillery piece or a vehicle up a hill, anything nasty they can dream up, you'll do. I'm not saying you have to grin from ear to ear and bear it without cursing the bastard who's giving the orders,' says an ex-trooper, 'but it helps. This is where you learn about being the Grey Man. He is the one nobody notices in a crowd. The Training Wing are looking for the loudmouth all the time, he is the first to go. Then comes the wimp, the one who can't hack it physically. And you'd be surprised at the Rambos who get chucked out, big strong athletic fellas who you'd think would fit the mould, the stereotype hard man. They're looking for that something extra, but then they can afford to be choosy, can't they?'

In some ways the outsider might reach the conclusion that SAS selection is extremely conservative in its preferences for a certain type of soldier, and in many ways this is true. An individual with strong opinions about soldiering or politics will not be welcomed by the SAS in the selection phase. But later, when a man has proved himself in the field as a badged member of the Regiment, his opinions will probably be stronger and the debates more passionate than in any other unit of the British Army.

Weapons training and familiarization plays a major part in the Regiment's choice of soldiers and any candidate who shows an inaptitude with them now will be immediately dropped from the course. In the final analysis, they are looking for good soldiers, so anyone who cannot prove himself to be effective with firearms is of little use. Training Wing sergeants are looking for the man with a natural dexterity who has outstanding coordination between hand and brain. Quick reactions and an ability to work well under stress are essential. At the end of the third week when just about everyone is more tired and weary than he has ever been before, the surviving candidates are dropped off from their transport at one of a number of remote locations in the Welsh hills for Long Drag. Training Wing does its utmost to disorientate the candidate by keeping details of the routes and rendezvous points quiet so that an element of surprise is included in the adventure. A paratrooper who passed SAS selection in the 1970s recalls:

You're there with your bergen on, sometimes you have to sit down to put it on, it is so heavy, that and the belt

38

kit. Then the sergeant points at an empty space on the map with a blade of grass and says '321, 123' – that's your map reference for the first rendezvous and you're off on your own trying to show enthusiasm. You're thinking to yourself, if I gallop off up the first hill, he'll give me brownie points, have a breather in the dead ground over the top, but it doesn't work like that. You're up against the clock and you have to set yourself a pace. That's the only way you'll get there in the time they allow you. It is probably then that you realize it is your own challenge, it's no longer you and them. You're doing this to prove something to yourself, a bit like running the marathon.

The twenty hours that candidates are given to complete Long Drag are remembered in a variety of ways, but no soldier who passed selection will ever forget it. 'Part of it is the knowledge that if you make it in the time you'll be classed as one of the fittest soldiers in the British Army, which in itself makes you feel pretty good. You feel like a competitor at the Olympic Games who just won the gold.'

However, for the man who reaches the final rendezvous in time the battle is not yet over, as before he can be accepted into the SAS he must face a series of gruelling escape and evasion tests. Dressed in Second World War battledress, the soldier is turned loose in a remote area and given a rendezvous point to reach. He will have been strip-searched to verify that he is not carrying any food, water or items such as a compass that might make his task less demanding. The search is extremely thorough and anyone who thinks he can hide any small item in his mouth or other orifice need not try. One man who passed the test swallowed a miniature brass button compass and retrieved it later. However, by then the exercise was over and he never got the chance to use it. To make matters worse, a hunter force is employed to track down the candidates. To encourage this group, a promise of leave is offered to the men who capture their prey. Here is an account of one man's more fortuitous experience:

On the first morning, after spending the night lost in the woods, I was soaked to the skin and the greatcoat I had on weighed a ton. I heard voices and was sure this was a Guards Battalion who were chasing me. You have the choice of taking off at top speed, or lying up. They were so close I dropped down on one knee and listened. I heard Welsh voices. They turned out to be Forestry Commission blokes who had just arrived in the wood with their chainsaws. When I sneaked a look and saw this guy opening his Thermos and another one carrying his bait box ['bait' is a North of England word for food, especially a packed lunch], I came out and said hallo. Got some odd looks. Must have given them a bit of a shock I guess. Told them 'SAS escape and evasion exercise. Got any scoff?' This old bugger poured me a brew and I sat for a chat and some sandwiches before having a fag and taking off again. They were quite useful as they told me where they had seen the soldiers on their drive-in. You need to be dead careful though as people living and working in the area usually tip off the DS if they see you. They are often close by hobnobbing with some local farmer while the farmer's wife is cooking them a nice hot stew while you're out there freezing your rocks off.

Most of the candidates will be picked up by the hunter force, but those who succeed in evading them face the same treatment on reaching their destination RV. Hooded and tied up, the prisoner is dragged to an interrogation room where he will spend hours facing solitude, sensory deprivation and 'white noise' in a variety of positions. He may stand for hours, naked and hooded, spread-eagled against a brick wall in the freezing cold with the occasional punch if he dares to move. His task is to resist the interrogators' questions and only reply with his name, rank and number. He may reply 'I cannot reply to that question,' but nothing else.

The men and women asking the questions are experts in their field, and know all the tricks of their skilful trade. Alone and usually freezing cold, the potential SAS soldier may hear screams or vicious barking dogs as he lies huddled in a corner, or hangs suspended by a rope from the ceiling. He has no idea of the time or how long this drama may last. An army doctor will check his physical condition from time to time, but, unless he admits defeat and gives up, the victim must, as one veteran says, 'Just hack it. The worst they can do is kill you, and you know they aren't going to do that.' Having said that, he admitted that at one point when he got a fierce kick in the kidneys he wondered whether the SAS might sometimes bury the odd recruit in an unmarked grave. As a result of the publication of several former SAS men's memoirs in recent times, many of the interrogation-phase techniques have been adapted and updated by the DS and Intelligence Corps personnel to keep candidates in the dark as to what happens, but the treatment they receive, though clearly harsh, has been proven to work for captured SAS men facing real interrogations.

'Andy McNab' (not his real name), who was captured behind Iraqi lines in the Gulf War admitted that he was able to survive his gruelling captivity and torture thanks to interrogation training. Recruits who have survived this far are now dispatched to the Parachute Regiment for their basic parachuting course. Having satisfied them that he is capable of jumping out of an aeroplane without 'freezing' in the door the SAS trooper enters the continuation training phase. 'After selection it's a bit of a doddle,' says one soldier. 'Jungle training which comes next can be grim though, and one or two blokes suffered badly during that. You get asked where you'd like to serve. HALO,[1] Mountain, Mobility or Boat Troop, but in the end they put you in the troop and in the squadron where they need the men the most.'

Having joined his troop of fifteen men and an officer, itself a sub-unit of one of the Regiment's 'Sabre' Squadrons, A, B, D, or G, the new man begins to learn the finer arts of SAS soldiering. This includes special SAS tactics, living off the land and learning an individual skill, which may encompass medical, communications, demolitions or language training. Despite all he has been through during selection, he is very much the new boy, and it will be months and often years before he is finally accepted by his peers. The new boy is, at this stage, usually in his middle to late twenties and perhaps already a junior NCO in his parent regiment. Since the day he arrived in Hereford to begin selection, his rank was taken away from him, and now as a humble trooper he is in for some more shocks.

During his first year of service in the SAS, assuming he lasts that long, his pay will be the same as the day he arrived, so if he was a sergeant he receives a sergeant's wage. After the first year, as if to add insult to injury, this is reduced to a corporal's pay. The logic behind this rule is that primarily the Regiment has to establish a pecking order in the ranks with the most experienced men receiving the top pay; but it is also, according to some, because it adds another 'sickener' to the equation, letting the new man know that he is only in Hereford

[1] HALO – high altitude low opening

under sufferance. The reality though is that the Ministry of Defence is unwilling to pay NCO salaries to more than 700 men. Ahead of the new trooper there is continuation training and at least one very specialized skill to learn. One corporal from A Squadron recalled his training as a patrol medic in the mid-1970s:

I was sent to the casualty department of a major hospital in West London to see life and death at the sharp end. The first Saturday night was mind-blowing with drunks bleeding and throwing up everywhere, mostly head and face wounds from pub fights at closing time. I got on really well with the doctors and nurses who I quickly learned had a marvellous way of taking it all in their stride. One or two I think were quite pleased to have a fit guy around to help them as they really do take some terrible abuse night after night. I was quite willing to mop the floor and make them a brew, watching all the time how they did things.

Then someone handed me a fresh juicy orange and a suture needle and suggested I practise putting stitches in. Before long this middle-aged drunk was brought in with blood pouring from a scalp wound and the nurses suggested I lend a hand to clean him up. Before I knew it I was suturing the wounds, no problem! The nurses kept making jokes, giggling and saying I was the hospital's head-wound expert. The bloke never knew he had been stitched by a trooper in the SAS, though the sutures were probably a bit crooked.

Medical courses like this continue with more practical, and a good deal of theoretical, training. There are visits to the operating theatre for a close-up view of surgeons at work, and while the emphasis will be on learning trauma management for gunshot and blast wounds, the SAS medic will at the end of the course also be able to cope with conditions like cardiac arrest and childbirth. He will learn that when he is called on to deal with battlefield casualties behind enemy lines the only person who is going to save a seriously wounded comrade is him, and if that means carrying out a surgical operation in the field, he is the one who will have to do it. The trooper's superiors will quickly find out whether he is right for the job, for it may be that one of the other specialized skills suits him better. The shock treatment described by the trooper above exists to find out quickly if the man can handle the sight of heavy bleeding and stay cool under stress.

The survival skills taught to SAS recruits are the product of many years of Regimental experience and are regarded by most special forces units as being the best in the world. Operating in the majority of cases behind the enemy's lines, an SAS man is expected to be able to live off the land for long periods without resupply, and the chances are he will be evading the enemy most of the time. Each stage of survival training is designed to encourage the new recruit to think for himself and use his initiative in problem-solving scenarios which may one day save his life and the lives of his comrades.

Most of the lectures on survival are held in the open air and are relaxed affairs with a good deal of friendly banter between instructors and troopers. The first lesson deals with the art of staying alive and how to cope with the stresses that will be encountered in a survival situation. Controlling anxiety, which is the most natural reaction when the human mind is faced with potential disaster, must be learnt, and a clear assessment of the situation is vital. Once the man has come to terms with his predicament he must waste no time in organizing and planning and his first priorities are water and shelter. Although a healthy man can survive for about three weeks without food, he can only last for three days without water. Every day that passes without nourishment he will become weaker, so each day the clock is running against him. If he is able to find a water supply, great care must be taken to sterilize it for at all costs he must avoid becoming ill. If there is no obvious source of water in rivers or streams he can dig in places where he finds green vegetation to locate a source, search in crevices or rocks or collect rain water in a container.

Once he has found water, searching for food in the wild is the next priority. Nature, he will learn, is there to help him, and no matter where he is, something can almost always be found to eat. It may grow above or in the ground like plants or tubers, it may crawl or walk, like insects, snakes and animals, swim in rivers or the sea or fly through the air. Trapping small wild animals like rabbits, stoats and weasels with a wire snare is taught by skilled gamekeepers who are delighted to pass on their vast knowledge of animal behaviour.

Snares, the recruit learns, work more effectively when buried for a while in the earth. Before handling them you should rub your hands in the ground to get rid of any human smells and set the traps, several of them at a time, on the animal's runs, being careful not to disturb the ground. To catch a rabbit the loop of the snare should be about 5 centimetres off the ground, or roughly the width of a cigarette packet.

Nature's indicators are there to help the survivor, and by checking fresh tracks and droppings he can establish whether an animal trail is being used. Have spiders' webs been recently broken? That would indicate that a small mammal had passed this way. By watching birds, bees and ants he can learn from his surroundings where likely sources of both water and food might be found, for wherever they are there is water to sustain them, perhaps trapped in a hollow, in the branches of a tree.

45

Bees rarely fly more than 6 kilometres from their hive so honey, and the people who collect it, may not be far away. And what about mushrooms? The SAS survival instructor collects a dozen or more fungi and gives a running commentary on each one, giving its Latin and common names and identifying it as edible or poisonous. Mushrooms, he tells the recruits, can be a sustaining form of easily found food if you know where to look, 'But unless you can positively identify them, leave them alone!' Knowing the difference between the *Boletus edulis* which is very tasty, and the *Amanita virosa* which is known more commonly as the destroying angel and can kill you, is rather important when your life is on the line, so the minds of most recruits are focusing clearly at this stage.

Learning how to slaughter and prepare animals is taught simply and clearly. A live sheep is led out into a clearing in the Herefordshire woods where an instructor straddles the animal, lifts its head and swiftly cuts its throat. First he lets the animal bleed, catching the blood in a bowl and explains to the students that this will come in handy later on for adding to soups and stews. The animal is strung up on an improvised gantry, then disembowelled and skinned. When the creature has been prepared the meat is then cooked by burying it with hot stones in a trench fire that has been burning for some time.

Similar skinning, plucking and cooking lessons are given for smaller animals and birds, including chickens. The instructor, chicken in hand, asks the recruits, 'How do you kill a chicken?' Most shout back that they would wring its neck or cut its throat. With typical panache, the instructor simply rips its head off with one sharp movement leaving the headless bird to flap and die. Although it may sound harsh to those of us who buy our food in the supermarket, this is the reality of survival, and there is no place in the SAS for the squeamish.

One of the most popular parts of the training course is fishing, for during this stage they will not only learn how to catch fish in survival situations but also enjoy the pleasures that can be found tickling trout and simply sitting quietly beside a stream in one of the most beautiful parts of England. An experienced angler leads them along the river bank explaining how fish behave, what they eat, and a dozen or more ways of catching them using everything from a bent safety pin to a plastic Coca-Cola bottle cut in half. Though few SAS men belong to major angling clubs, many will spend their later years enjoying the tranquillity of the river banks, and taking the occasional trout or salmon from the waters.

The building of shelters is taught intensively, from the simplest basha using a poncho or tarpaulin to extremely complex affairs using cut logs or blocks of turf. In woodland, trainees learn how to cut and bend a tree to make a watertight shelter for the night, and how to make and rig an improvised hammock or stretcher using old plastic fertilizer bags which, with poles fed through, will support a man's weight. Keeping warm means having the ability to make fire, and as they say in the Regiment, 'One match, one fire'. They also say that there are many ways to start a fire, and using matches is not the only way. Others include flint struck against steel, wire wool touching the terminals of a battery, sodium chlorate or potassium chlorate mixed three to one with sugar, or if none of these is available, there is always the Stone Age fire bow where hard wood is drilled into soft, creating eventually a puff of smoke and, if you are lucky, flame. Field dressings, of which the SAS man can never have enough, make excellent tinder for this method, as does cotton wool or bark from the silver birch.

Before completing the Combat Survival Course, as it is correctly known, students will have covered topics which include health and hygiene in the field, navigation, improvised weapons, safe river crossings, edible and medicinal plants, and observation awareness. Depending on which troop they have been allocated to, HALO, Amphibious, Mountain or Mobility, the new man begins an intensive course in his specialist field. For those in the HALO troops there is a six-week parachuting course which, after some basic free-fall jumps from 12,000 feet, will introduce them to the unforgettable experience of plunging from 25,000 feet or more from the back of a Hercules transport aircraft while breathing oxygen from a bottle. An NCO who served with one of the HALO troops in the 1980s advised, with typical cynicism: 'Always a good idea to take some loose change in your pocket. Half the time during the night drops you'd land miles off course when you were aiming for the camp. You ended up trapesing off down the lane carrying your chute and looking for a phone box.' Few who embark on this course take it lightly as the simplest of mistakes, such as losing stability during the free-fall descent, can lead to a misfunction of the parachute canopy's safe deployment and lead to a 'high-speed Valhalla', instant death.

Today's SAS parachutists prefer to use steerable chutes, rectangular affairs similar to those favoured by civilian free-fallers. GQ Parachutes Ltd in Glamorgan manufactures the GQ-360 Advanced Ram Air System parachute which can deliver a paratrooper with a total weight of 160 kilos (paratrooper and his kit) from 25,000 feet. The GQ-360, in service with Britain's special forces today, is also used by French elite troops such as the Compagnie de Recherche et d'Action en Profondeur (CRAPs) who, like the SAS, carry out part of their training at Pau, in south-west France. During HALO and HAHO (high altitude high opening) jumps the SAS trooper's bergen is inverted and slung across the back of his thighs, making free-fall descents both awkward and hazardous for he must assume a delicate spread-eagled posture as he leaves the aircraft. If he begins to tumble, he may find it impossible to correct his fall, and releasing the chute in this state can quite easily end in disaster. To avoid breaking the symmetry of his body during descent, a special canopy-deployment system that functions on barometric pressure like an aircraft's altimeter, opens his chute automatically, and at a safe height which can be pre-set before jumps.

So what does it feel like to parachute from 25,000 feet wearing oxygen apparatus into enemy territory at night? Landing at night and being unable to see the ground clearly presents serious hazards, and the tried and tested paratrooper's technique of 'bend the knees, legs together' leaves a lot to be desired as the ground, wherever it is, is rushing up to meet you. Once the canopy is safely deployed the bergen, which may weigh more than 50 kilos, is lowered on a strap, so this is the first item to hit the ground. Defence 'boffins' came up with the idea of incorporating a signal device that would warn the paratrooper he only had a couple of seconds before terra firma arrived, but this, like the use of fluorescent cyalume sticks attached to the bergen, did little to make night parachuting easier. The drawback with the use of cyalume sticks was that the enemy could see them glowing on their way down.

Members of the Amphibious Troops, more commonly called Boat Troops, meanwhile, are learning about the technicalities of closed-circuit diving apparatus which, unlike civilian equivalents, leave no bubbles, and the expertise required in handling Rigid Raiders (fast amphibious landing craft) and Klepper canoes (collapsible two-man canoes for special forces which can be deployed from a submarine for covert operations). The Royal Marines Special Boat Service (SBS) which today comes under the same directorate as the SAS at the Ministry of Defence (MoD), is on hand to assist with training.

A recent decision by the MoD enabling SBS personnel who preferred not to further their diving careers to cross over to SAS duties, if they were considered capable of passing SAS selection, has brought the two elite forces closer together. Submersible craft capable of travelling long distances to their targets underwater are used for covert insertion of SAS and SBS teams into enemy waters and for the reconnaissance of their beaches.

For those who join one of the SAS's four Mountain Troops, the adventure and the danger facing them is just as hard as the Regiment's HALO team members' activities, and sometimes more so. Not only are they expected to climb in conditions that would drive the keenest civilian mountaineer down into the valley for shelter, they are also supposed to fight. Basic climbing techniques using kernmantel ropes, chocks, slings, friends and pitons are taught and great attention is paid to knot-tying so that even in the dark the mountain trooper can belay himself to a rock or tie a figure-of-eight on his rope until these skills become second nature to him.

He will have the opportunity to find out whether he can stay alive in a snow hole in northern Norway where temperatures can drop to minus 40 degrees Celsius without counting in the windchill factor. Learning about mountain weather conditions, where in the course of a few hours he may see blazing sunshine turning to white-out blizzards, is of life-saving importance, and he will learn how to recognize and deal with hypothermia and frostbite.

Abseiling in the normal manner where you control your descent on the rope, and carrying out the same manoeuvre head-first will become routine pastimes on Welsh and Scottish crags. Like many of his regiment's predecessors he will probably take part in civilian-style mountaineering expeditions to the Alps, the Dolomites or the Pyrenees, or like ex-Regiment soldiers John 'Brummie' Stokes and Michael 'Bronco' Lane, travel halfway across the world and try to climb Everest or K2.

The operation of the Regiment's vehicles and all overland transport is the domain of the Mobility Troops, also know as Landrover Troops. With their long-wheelbase Landrovers, Range Rovers and Unimogs they are the experts in cross-country driving in all terrains, from the deserts of Saudi Arabia to the Arctic Circle, and with the progress in satellite navigation and passive night vision equipment, today's mobile SAS patrols can go virtually anywhere at any time and still know exactly where they are. They are experts at handling Landrovers, most especially the custom-made long-wheelbase Pink Panther designed primarily for desert operations; they also operate a range of off-road trail motorbikes which are used for reconnaissance missions. During the Gulf War some of these motorcyclists played an invaluable role operating as forward scouts for Landrover patrols.[2] With their vast fleet of Landrovers which can be fitted with general purpose machine guns (GPMGs), Browning .50s or the Mark 19/Model 3 grenade launcher, today's SAS mobile

[2] Trooper David Denbury, MM, was killed in action in 1991 during one of these missions.

patrols pack a punch that would have impressed even David Stirling.

By the time his induction training period is over, the new trooper will have been in 22 SAS Regiment for a little less than two years. When and if the candidate passes this phase, he may begin to feel accepted by the Regiment. Badging of the few who succeed is a casual affair in the CO's office, and having been welcomed into 22 SAS the successful man is handed, or more often thrown his sand-coloured beret and badge. For now, in the eyes of the Directing Staff and the other members of his squadron he is ready for action.

> In the SAS it would be fair to say that the training never really finishes. You're learning something all the time and perhaps operating in regions of the world that are new to you. A guy may have spent a lot of time in the mountains with plenty of sunshine on his back and become an expert living out in the field, then suddenly he is working the back streets of Belfast. A short while later he is catching fish with traps in the Far East or maybe learning how to handle small boats off a coral reef. There is never a dull moment, though of course some blokes can age pretty fast doing it.

The opportunity for action and actual combat for the newly badged SAS man depends entirely on world events, and it may be that months or even years go by before he is sent on a combat mission. That being said, the chances are pretty high that he will see action within a short time of his joining the Regiment, for SAS headquarters (the Headshed) wants to know how he behaves under fire in his new troop. His military career up until he joined the SAS has been carefully studied by the Training Wing, but this will not impress the Regiment's hardened NCOs. The trooper who has a reputation for being heroic or a 'hard man' in his previous soldiering career is subject to closer scrutiny than the one who shows an element of humility before his peers. A HALO trooper recalled:

> You think when they throw you the beret, that's it – you're in. The reality is you're only there until you either cock up on an operation or you cross over the line of acceptability. In my case it was a few years into my service with A Squadron when I crossed the line. It was in a pub in Hereford and this officer's wife was giving me a hard time. Everyone was well pissed. Something she was saying was getting my back up and I really felt like giving her a bunch of fives in the mouth. I controlled my feelings for long enough, then I just spat at her in the face. Before I knew what was happening it was time to see the Colonel, and not long after that it was RTU [returned to unit].

Unlike the paratrooper who has just won his Pegasus Wings, the newly badged SAS trooper is forbidden from parading around his home town in uniform which means that his casual friends and neighbours will rarely know that he is in Britain's most elite regiment. With the beret comes the understanding that from now on he will watch his back and never talk about operations or fellow members of the SAS to strangers. The penalty for infringement of this strict rule is instant RTU. This is one reason that even off duty or on leave the men spend a considerable amount of their time together.

Wives and girlfriends are often quickly invited by one of the officers' wives to join the social circle that brings these women closer together which, in a close-knit community like the small city of Hereford, means that almost everyone knows everyone else.

It takes a while for each SAS trooper to settle into his new job and for most of the time he will be too busy to notice the time passing. Fitness is considered to be essential and whenever he is in Hereford he will be expected to train each day to keep himself in shape. If this all sounds a little extreme, there are some advantages which the new man will soon discover. Hereford and the area surrounding it boasts some of the finest pubs in England, and the social life for an unattached and fit-looking young man who has a reasonably decent wage coming in each month is excellent. The fact that for the majority a large amount of their income will be blown away on buying rounds of drinks for their comrades is just something they have to get used to.

THREE

RENAISSANCE OF A REGIMENT

In the peaceful graveyard at Saint Martin's church near the SAS camp in Hereford lie the bodies of some of the Regiment's dead, those who failed to 'beat the clock', and a stained-glass window inside the church showing scenes from typical SAS operations lists the campaigns in which its members have fought, often at the time in great secrecy. The list is long and includes Malaya (1950–59), Oman (1958–9), Borneo (1962–6), Southern Arabia (1964–7), Oman (1970–76), the Falkland Islands (1982), Iraq (1991), and Northern Ireland. Behind each gravestone there lies a story, usually of heroism in the face of the enemy, but sometimes, as in the case of the Falklands campaign, of a disaster that nobody could have predicted.[1] Soldiering in the SAS, it must be said, is a very dangerous business.

At the end of the Second World War the British government saw little use for such an elite and specialized regiment as the SAS and in 1945 it was disbanded, much

[1] Twenty men serving or attached to the SAS died when their Sea King helicopter crashed into the South Atlantic during a night cross-decking operation on 19 May 1982 during the Falklands War.

to the annoyance of David Stirling and the men who had served with him in some of the fiercest campaigns of the war. It was clearly a short-sighted decision taken, as Stirling would have said, by 'grey-suits' in the corridors of Whitehall, but two years later Whitehall made a concession. In 1947, a Territorial unit, 21 Special Air Service Regiment (Artists' Rifles) was created in London. In fact, the 'Artists' were not new.

The Artists' Rifles had been founded in 1859 from a group of painters, architects, musicians, engravers and actors as part of the Volunteer Corps which was raised to face a threatened invasion by the French. Their members included several famous names, William Holman Hunt, John Everett Millais, Frederic, Lord Leighton (a President of the Royal Academy) and William Morris, and later Noël Coward and Barnes Wallis, among many others. During the First World War, its members had won eight VCs, fifty-two DSOs and 822 MCs, among other awards.

Between the world wars Artists took part in the leading shooting competitions and excelled as marksmen. In 1939 they became an officer training organization. In 1950 numerous colonial wars were happening around the world, and Britain's interests in Malaya were threatened by a force of 10,000 communist guerrillas supported by Indonesia. A reign of terror existed in the country and there were countless murders and terrorist attacks against expatriate Britons.

A former SAS officer, Mike Calvert, who had commanded a Chindit brigade behind Japanese lines in Burma during the war, wrote an assessment of the conflict suggesting that the only way to turn the tide in Malaya was by using a force of highly trained and motivated soldiers who could 'win the hearts and minds' of the indigenous people. Calvert believed that Britain's leaders had failed to understand the nature of the war, and that, with the creation of a jungle-trained force which could operate deep in hostile country, it might be possible to deny the enemy freedom of movement. The guerrillas relied on local Malayans to feed and support them, often using tactics of terror. Denying them this support would bring the guerrillas out into the open where they could be dealt with. By offering villagers humanitarian aid and medical help, Calvert believed he could win.

Towards the end of the Second World War, the Special Operations Executive had carried out numerous operations in the Far East, and had trained some of the guerrillas Britain was now fighting.[2] In 1945 the regimental adjutant of the SAS, Major C. E. 'Dare' Newell had carried out several highly dangerous and delicate missions in Malaya as part of 'Force 136'. Newell's practical knowledge of the jungle and his understanding of the local situation now became vital to the planning of the Malayan campaign.

Mike Calvert created the Malayan Scouts (SAS), and began recruiting experienced soldiers from Force 136, the SOE, and 21 SAS (Artists' Rifles) which included a handful of David Stirling's 'Originals'. Calvert's force was now given an identity and organized into squadrons, his original volunteers becoming A Squadron, the Territorials (Artists) becoming B Squadron, and a unit from Rhodesia (now Zimbabwe) forming C Squadron.[3]

[2] SOE had trained Malayan communists to fight against the Japanese during the Second World War.

[3] C Squadron (Rhodesia) continued to exist until the end of the Rhodesian war, but was known as the 'Lost Legion' following Ian Smith's declaration of UDI in 1964 but, despite being cut off from the SAS 'family', Rhodesian members retained their close links with Hereford. A telegram sent to C Squadron at the time stated 'C Squadron will remain always in the Orbat [Order of Battle] of the SAS Regiment.'

The nine-year guerrilla war was fought mainly in primary jungle and it was here that the SAS developed and refined the art of tree-jumping. To insert their patrols, each man would parachute with 100 feet of hessian rope. Once he had crashed feet first through the upper tree canopy his chute would snag on the branches and he would come to a halt. Then, in theory, it was a simple case of releasing the chute's harness and lowering himself down the rope. Of course, in practice things did not always go the way they should and there were some horrific injuries. At the end of the Malayan Emergency this method was abandoned as being unnecessarily dangerous. Malaya was a valuable training ground, and the men who served there quickly sharpened their jungle skills. Learning to move silently and extremely slowly, and to blend into the vegetation, they developed patrol techniques that have been passed on to less elite infantry regiments. The principle of the four-man brick remained for most operations, and a wide range of weapons including the shotgun were brought into service.

SAS men soon discovered that the soldier who shoots fast and accurately, but most importantly, who shoots first, will live to tell the tale. Spraying the jungle haphazardly, a popular technique employed later by thousands of American GIs in Vietnam, was a waste of time and bullets. One reason for not doing so was the simple fact that leaves and branches, no matter how flimsy, had the effect of deflecting the outgoing rounds, and the chances of effectively hitting a moving target in the heat of a firefight while shooting weapons on automatic were slim. Carefully aimed shots not only neutralized the enemy but also enabled the soldier to conserve ammunition, a key factor in the heat of the jungle where weight is of fundamental importance.

Patrolling techniques employed in the jungle were completely different from those used by SAS men elsewhere. Moving silently under the cover of darkness and lying up in the daytime, traditional procedure for special forces, was quickly seen as being impracticable. Patrols were carried out in daylight and just before last light, the men would make camp, posting sentries to watch for enemy activity. Sleeping in a tropical rainforest requires particular skills, and SAS soldiers rapidly learned the practical techniques of shelter building using A-frames and hammocks. The acquisition of jungle skills became of paramount importance and some of the men who had operated behind Japanese lines in the Second World War were invaluable to the creation of the reborn SAS. Like Stirling, 'Mad Mike' Calvert had joined the Scots Guards at the outbreak of the war and following a three-year posting to Burma where he had fought the Japanese with the deep-penetration Chindit groups, commanded the SAS in north-west Europe until disbandment in 1945. Calvert's knowledge of jungle warfare and the specialized skills that go with it were quickly passed on to the men serving in Malaya. Those techniques became a part of the SAS's training programme and their finer arts are still taught today.

During the Malayan campaign the SAS served with distinction in an environment in which few armies could survive, facing not only a ruthless and cunning enemy but also disease and extreme physical hardship. In the first seven years of operation, twenty-eight SAS soldiers died in some of the fiercest and the most gruelling combat that the Regiment has ever faced. They had, however re-established themselves as a regiment in the British Army's order of battle, and those who served there were going to make sure that the SAS remained.

This became more likely in 1962 when SAS soldiers were deployed on a four-year campaign in Borneo, and the two defunct squadrons were restored. In the following years, Conservative and Labour governments became increasingly aware of the advantages that a small and effective secret military force could provide, and numerous countries friendly to the United Kingdom made it known to British diplomats that their security was at risk, and that in return for British military aid now, there could be major advantages later. Needless to say more than one of these friendly nations was worried that its less than respectable regime would be subject to a left-wing coup or a family feud. This was the height of the Cold War, and Britain, like the United States and nations with colonial, material or simply friendly interests, viewed the growing tide of communism with dismay and foreboding. The discreet style of SAS operations and its soldiers' code of self-enforced secrecy meant then, and means today, that a certain 'deniability' could be brought into the equation.

The creation of small-unit British Army Training Teams (BATTs) which could be sent out from the United Kingdom to instruct foreign military forces became the ideal solution. Not only would they make indigenous forces more effective, they also offered Whitehall the chance of putting British military eyes and ears on friendly foreign soil and close to those of the less friendly. A detailed situation report submitted to the Ministry of Defence in London by the commanding officer of an SAS BATT was a valuable document in the hands of a defence attaché, and enabled ministers from both sides of the political divide to plan foreign policy.

This led inevitably to the involvement of the Secret Intelligence Service (MI6) in SAS affairs, and there were some in the Intelligence community then, as there are today, who began to look on the Regiment as a tailor-made and superbly skilled spy force. SAS commanders during and since the Second World War vigorously resisted successive overtures by Britain's spymasters to involve themselves in 'regimental business', just as David Stirling had resisted the SOE in wartime. This does not mean, however, that the Regiment is not involved in MI6 or MI5 operations, or that senior ranks in the SAS do not fraternize occasionally with Britain's espionage and security agencies.

In 1962, shortly after David Stirling had returned to England after his post-war years in southern Africa, he discovered that his services were still in demand by Her Majesty's Government, though he would never again need his battledress. Having maintained close ties with influential friends in London he was invited to recruit a covert force to assist the Imam of Yemen, who had just been overthrown in an Egyptian-backed coup. The British protectorate of Aden to the north was under threat, and Stirling enthusiastically recruited a group of ex-SAS officers for the operation. This was to be the beginning of a long and very discreet relationship, which contiunues today, between Whitehall's corridors of power and ex-members of the Regiment. Although the Yemen adventure failed in its long-term strategy when Britain withdrew from Aden in the late 1960s, Egyptian forces were severely weakened by Stirling's operation. In 1967, when Israel was fighting for survival in the Six Day War, large numbers of Egypt's best troops, pilots and aircraft, thanks to Stirling, were deployed in the Yemen.

Britain's interests in the oil-rich Gulf states and alliances with their rulers led to the deployment of SAS BATT in Oman and other regions of Arabia through the late 1950s right up to the present day. In 1972, fewer than a dozen members of B Squadron who had just completed their tour in Oman and were due to return home the next day, came under attack from an over-whelming rebel force of Adoo tribesmen at the small coastal town of Mirbat. In the ensuing battle, the defenders fought one of the most courageous actions in the Regiment's history, and it was here that the SAS's Fijian mythology was born. Labalaba and Takavesi who had joined the British Army from Fiji in the 1960s, heroically fought off the charging Adoo tribesmen by loading and firing a 25-pounder field gun straight into the enemy. At one point Labalaba was firing it single-handed, which requires almost unimaginable strength and determination. Backed up by their comrades firing a mortar, machine guns and rifles, and led by a young SAS officer, Mike Kealey, they managed to hold off the attackers until air support and reinforcements arrived. Although not the only casualty of the battle, Labalaba remains one of 22 SAS Regiment's greatest warriors who failed to 'beat the clock'.

By the time the first American Green Beret 'advisors' landed in Vietnam in 1963 a number of other Special Air Service regiments had been formed, with Rhodesians, Australians and New Zealanders joining the SAS family. This was to offer added advantages to the British-based 22 SAS, who now had colleagues in far-flung places with whom they could compare ideas and training methods. In the late 1960s and early 1970s Australian and New Zealand troops were supporting American special forces in Vietnam, though in most cases they operated totally independently of the Green Berets, Seals, LURPs, Rangers and other elite US units serving there. Whether British-based SAS soldiers ever set foot on Vietnamese soil is a question that has long gone unanswered by either Britain's Ministry of

Defence or the men themselves. The most likely answer is that then, as now, SAS men are often invited to 'drop in and have a look' at a particular theatre of war without being committed operationally.

Cross-training between other SAS units and those based in the United Kingdom continues today, and it is not unusual for an Australian or New Zealander to be found among the ranks of the British SAS on operations in some remote and secret war.

Australian SAS operations and training are directed from Northam on the outskirts of Perth in Western Australia, while the New Zealanders maintain a base at Waiouru on North Island near the Kaimanawa Mountains. Though their weaponry, combat fatigues and other equipment is slightly different from those of their Hereford cousins (Australians use the Austrian Steyr rifle and a clever computer-designed camouflage that really works in the bush) many of the training and operational techniques are similar, though climatic differences can be a shock to SAS men who cross-train during exchanges. Maori volunteers played an important role in the formation of the Australasian SAS regiments, bringing extraordinary tracking and survival skills into those ranks. Consequently, the majority of Australasian SAS men today have a natural and highly developed ability to live off the land and survive in some of the hardest territory on the planet. That said, some still find it hard coming to terms with the very special and extremely tiring barren hills and inclement weather that can be found most weekends in the Brecon Beacons.

During the Rhodesian war, members of the the 'lost legion' who had previously been C Squadron in the SAS order of battle developed their own gruelling selection system and a number of Hereford veterans joined them. Among the most courageous was Scotsman Peter McAleese who was with them on a number of hair-raising cross-border search and destroy missions in Mozambique and Zambia before leaving to work firstly with Rhodesian Special Branch, then the South African Defence Force (SADF). Described by some who know him well as the ultimate professional soldier, McAleese's reputation for toughness had reached the Rhodesians before he even arrived in the country. Constantly bullied by a senior NCO who insisted the Scotsman did not know how to march properly, McAleese did what all good SAS men do in such situations and knocked the aggressive sergeant out.

Insertion into enemy territory was usually carried out by French-built Alouette or US UH-1 Huey helicopters[4] although on some major operations the Rhodesian Air Force used Second World War DC3 Dakotas to drop parachute troops from as low as 800 feet, and sometimes less. The Rhodesian SAS were the last members of the SAS 'family' to permit their members to wear their SAS wings (normally worn on the sleeve) on their chest after being blooded in battle, a tradition last approved by Stirling in the Western Desert. When the war in Rhodesia finally ended and Robert Mugabe won that country's elections, there was no longer a place for the Rhodesian SAS. This was understandable as most of its members had planned to assassinate him as the war was coming to a close. C Squadron's regimental clock tower, almost identical to the one in Hereford, was smuggled to South Africa in a typical SAS-style covert operation where it remains today. Some of the C Squadron troopers, NCOs and officers who fought in the closing stages of that war

---

[4] Some UH-1 Hueys were imported from Israel during the Rhodesian War, passing through South Africa, and thus effectively breaking UN sanctions.

were in their twenties when Rhodesia became Zimbab-we, and South Africa welcomed many of them who 'took the gap'[5] and went south. Soon they were carrying out covert operations in Namibia, Angola and Mozam-bique for the South African army, many of them having joined the SADF's elite Recce Commando units.

By the mid-1970s it was clear that the Regiment was here to stay. There were now four Sabre Squadrons, A, B, D, and G, each consisting of seventy-two operational SAS soldiers who were divided into four troops of sixteen men. Each troop was further sub-divided into four teams of four, the standard British Army section or 'brick'. Each squadron contained HALO, Mountain, Boat and Mobil-ity (Landrover) specialists, sixteen men in each, with a major in command who was supported by a captain. There was also a Headquarters Staff permanently based at Bradbury Lines (later Stirling Lines) in Hereford, a research and development wing known as Ops Research, and a cadre of NCOs who were responsible for training and recruitment, the Directing Staff (DS).

Because officers only served three-year tours with the SAS, there was a feeling which still exists today that the Regiment was run by its sergeants. Of course this is complete nonsense, as the SAS's brigadier is the man in charge, backed up by his second-in-command, a colonel, who is in turn backed up by his majors and captains. The fact that some NCOs may have spent twenty or more years in Hereford does, however, mean that they usually know much more about the workings of the SAS machine than any officer ever can. To add to the confu-sion, a tradition has developed during the Regiment's history of not wearing any rank slides, stripes, pips or crowns on combat clothing, so that personnel from another regiment, or corps, or from the Royal Navy,

[5] Rhodesian term for running down south to South Africa.

Royal Marines or Royal Air Force, really have no idea if they are talking to a major or a trooper.

Years ago it was usually possible to identify the officers from other ranks simply by listening to their accents, but in today's army, unless the officer belongs, for example, to the Household Cavalry and speaks with a veritable plum in his mouth, it is not so easy. This of course enables SAS men to get away with absolute murder when operating in conjunction with other regiments. On exercises in Norway or Germany it normally suffices for a trooper to mutter 'SAS' to a superior officer who has questioned his actions, to be left alone with an 'Oh, right . . . sorry'. Because the world in which they live is 'Secret, Restricted, and for their eyes only', most officers outside the SAS, although they would very much like to know what a particular group of men is up to, have been taught not to ask. This can lead to rumour and misinformation, often inspired and nurtured by the Regiment's soldiers themselves who enjoy a good joke. Some foreign armies, the Americans for example, find this highly confusing and cannot understand how the system can possibly work in practice. The use of Christian names, or more often nicknames, which abounds in SAS ranks is also a source of confusion to outsiders, but the traditional 'Boss' when a soldier is addressing his officer, is common parlance and perfectly acceptable unless a man is up on a charge. When this happens the Regiment and its members return to 'good old army bull', and there is plenty of drill, screaming and marching at double-time.

The Special Boat Service whose title has a habit of changing from time to time, and is frequently mis-named in newspapers as the Special Boat Squadron, is the SAS's nautical brother-at-arms. Recruiting from the Royal Marines, it is a small and very specialized force dedicated

66

to sea-borne operations using Klepper canoes, inflatable craft, Rigid Raiders and submersible boats. Following their daring and very successful Second World War operations in the Mediterranean where they carried out harrying raids on the enemy from the sea, it was inevitable that they would have a special place in today's British special forces.

Increasingly, their work is becoming more closely linked with that of the SAS in spite of ancient rivalries between two old adversaries, the Parachute Regiment (there are many paras in the SAS) and the Royal Marines. Now under the command of the same directorate at the Ministry of Defence, the SAS and the SBS work in harmony, whatever the odd paratrooper might tell you. The decision to commit selected members of the SAS to anti-terrorist operations in Great Britain and Northern Ireland did not occur overnight. Veterans of guerrilla warfare in Aden, Kenya and elsewhere offered valuable advice on practical methods of dealing with 'war on your doorstep', as historian and author Tony Geraghty called it in his excellent book *Who Dares Wins*. The part that modern technology would play was at the time unforeseen, and there was certainly a reluctance in all military units to advance into the computer age. Covert operations against terrorists then lacked the sophisticated equipment that is available today, very few concealable miniature communications systems worked effectively, and worst of all they could not be relied on. The same could be said for weapons and other equipment that early counter-revolutionary warfare-trained (CRW) soldiers were equipped with at the time. Gradually that situation changed, and it was not long before Hereford boasted its own specially equipped and dedicated anti-terrorist unit known as the Pagoda Troop. Today's CRW men operate in the shadows from their Hereford base, and they are ready at a moment's notice to deploy anywhere in the United Kingdom to face a terrorist threat.

David Stirling watched the transition of his Regiment with fascination, and he was always on hand to offer advice or listen to accounts of the latest SAS innovations. Several of the most experienced officers and NCOs joined him on their retirement from the Regiment, and throughout the latter part of his life he ran a number of security consultancy companies from an impressive office at 22 South Audley Street in London's Mayfair. While a steady stream of politicians, foreign diplomats, and senior officers flowed through the office's reception room, upstairs in the building's attic there could often be found a hungover or jet-lagged veteran from the Battle of Mirbat curled up in his 'green maggot,'[6] or a cardboard carton containing intravenous drips for the wounded in some faraway battle. The new Special Air Service had come a long way since its creation, but there was now absolutely no doubt in the minds of the men who sipped their malt whisky in Mayfair with 'D.S.' that it was here to stay.

[6] Sleeping bag.

FOUR

—

WEAPONS AND EQUIPMENT

During their years of service, the accumulated skills acquired by SAS personnel can become quite formidable, and those who remain to serve as senior NCOs are frequently offered slightly less exhausting jobs within the Regiment as they grow older. They are still required to maintain a high standard of physical fitness, and the majority are still delighted to give the younger troopers stiff competition on the Welsh hills or elsewhere. Their knowledge is put to good use, and while some finish their careers as Directing Staff (DS), others may find themselves involved in research and development of the Regiment's vehicles, weapons and equipment.

The wealth of knowledge in their specialized fields is encouraged and nurtured by the Headshed in Hereford, and usually the only restriction placed on the activities of Operations Research (Ops Research) is financial. For example, when a particular item of kit is made available for approval, a small group of experienced NCOs will try it out in all weathers, find the worst possible scenario in which the item might be used, and then abuse it to the point of destruction. Knives, radios, bullet-proof vests, helmets, bergens, webbing, vehicles and firearms will be pushed beyond the manufacturers' limits to find out if they are not only soldier-proof, but SAS-proof.

Kit that survives, and not much does, finds its way into the quartermaster's store where it may be stowed away for years until such an item is needed for a particular task. To suggest that the SAS has an unlimited budget (it does not) or that the Regiment can use anything it wants would be untrue, but they certainly have more freedom in the choice of equipment than any other British regiment.

The Armoury

In the 1960s and 1970s weapons most commonly used were the standard issue self-loading rifle (SLR) known to the military as the L1A1 (a semi-automatic, in that it can only fire one shot at a time, although the spent case is automatically ejected and replaced with a new round), the bolt-action Lee Enfield L42A1 sniper's rifle, the general-purpose machine gun (GPMG or 'gimpy'), the Sterling sub-machine gun (SMG), and the Browning Hi-Power pistol. Added to this armoury and used most effectively during the Iranian embassy siege was the Heckler & Koch MP5K sub-machine gun. All of these, apart from the Heckler & Koch, were standard weapons which fired either 7.62mm or 9mm cartridges and were in use by other units of the army, but with the introduction of the smaller 5.56mm round developed for the American AR-15 and its successor the M-16, SAS soldiers became increasingly attracted to the new, lower calibre weapons. The M-16 has the advantage of being extremely light; without its sling or magazine the Colt Commando, for example, weighs only 2.78 kilos, compared with the SLR which is almost twice the weight, and the capability of firing bursts with the lighter cartridge is clearly an advantage.

Teething troubles encountered by American troops who used the M-16 extensively in Vietnam (they rarely cleaned their rifles as often as they should have done) were ironed out by SAS men who found the weapon to be extremely accurate, with a little practice. The only disadvantage they could find was that occasionally the 5.56mm bullet lacked the 'stopping power' of the heavier 7.62mm round used in their old SLRs and sniping rifles. To resolve this, a variety of other rifles were tested and in their armoury today those interested in firearms would see a wide variety of other weapons such as the Heckler & Koch G-3K carbine with its retractable butt stock, the HK-53 and the Swiss-made Sig Sauer range of handguns. As a rule the SAS have always preferred the so-called 'automatic'[1] handguns rather than revolvers owing to their extremely rapid rates of fire and speedy magazine changes.

Added to the armoury today are some of the latest weapons currently in production such as the NATO Minimi 5.56mm light machine gun and the M203 40mm grenade launcher, which is fixed under the barrel of the M-16 rifle. The 203 has probably become the most popular weapon for general use in the SAS today with its dual-purpose capability of fully automatic rifle and grenade launcher which operates on a single-shot breechloading system. With an effective range of up to 400 metres, a wide choice of grenades can be chosen for specific targets. These include high explosive (HE), high explosive airbust (HE airbust), high-explosive smokeless and flashless, high explosive dual purpose (HEDP), plus a variety of parachute flares and practice rounds.

---

[1] Such weapons are not true *automatics*. They are *self-loading* pistols, and work in much the same way as the SLR.

The M203, built by JC Manufacturing Inc., Minneapolis, replaced the American M-79 grenade launcher during the Vietnam war, and like its predecessor quickly found favour with the Regiment.

Used to good effect during the Gulf War was another 40mm grenade launcher, the Mark 19 Model 3. Manufactured by Saco, a subsidiary of the US Maremont Corporation, this is an air-cooled, blow-back machine gun capable of firing a variety of grenades (including armour-piercing), either a single round at a time or fully automatic. In fully auto mode its rate of fire is an incredible 325 to 375 rounds per minute, though in combat a belt-link of twenty or fifty rounds is normally used. Mounted on the ground or in a vehicle (in the Gulf War the SAS fired them from their Landrovers) the Mark 19 has an effective range of 1,600 metres.

In the 1970s the Regiment's snipers favoured the bolt-action 7.62mm Enfield L42A1 magazine rifle, which was in fact a converted Number 4 Lee-Enfield .303 rifle. Today's marksmen have at their disposal a wide range of weapons to choose from, and one of the most effective is the Accuracy International PM 7.62mm bolt-action sniper rifle which is constructed on an aluminium frame. Weighing a little over 6 kilos and designated the L96A1, the PM has a stainless steel barrel and is furnished with a Schmidt & Bender 6 ¥ 42 telescopic sight. For counter-terrorism work, a more powerful 12 x optical sight or a zoom 2.5¥ to 10¥ telescope are available. Manufactured in Portsmouth, the PM is capable of hitting a target with the first round at up to 600 metres and can lay down accurate harassing fire up to 1,000 metres. A noise suppressor can be fitted to reduce the sniper's signature, and the rifle comes with a fully adjustable, lightweight bipod. The evolution of the SAS from an elite commando unit into a specially trained, multi-role force which is also reponsible for anti-terrorist operations has not gone unnoticed by the arms and equipment suppliers at home and abroad.

The close links established over the years with US Special Forces, most especially Delta Force, has enabled SAS personnel to see at close hand the massive American arsenal of weaponry and other kit, and in most cases try it out. This special relationship is encouraged by both sides, as frequently SAS men will develop and improve such equipment for uses which their American allies had not foreseen. Also, the more relaxed attitude in the United States towards sports shooting and gun clubs has enabled past and present SAS personnel to mix with some of America's top military and civilian competition shooters whose accuracy and skill with firearms is renowned. With their usual reluctance to appear in the public gaze, the men from Hereford will rarely be seen taking part in the world's pistol or rifle shooting competitions, though the Regiment could boast (though it does not) several world-class competition marksmen.

Stun Grenades
In addition to the Heckler & Koch MP5 series of submachine guns with 30-round magazines, and Remington 870 or Winchester pump-action shotguns which are carried by the Regiment's SP teams, the stun grenade or 'flash-bang' also plays a valuable role. Invented by the SAS, these magnesium-based explosive devices create a blinding flash, noise and smoke to disorientate an adversary, and have a devastating effect on the nerves of those not accustomed to them. Designed to disable and traumatize anyone who is near them, these devices explode with such ferocity that, in most cases, electric lights in a room will be blown out by the shockwave.

Stun grenades, which first came to the public's notice at the Iranian Embassy siege in London in 1980, were first used in an operation by the SAS in October 1977 when the Regiment's German equivalent, GSG-9 stormed a hi-jacked Lufthansa airliner in Mogadishu, Somalia. Assisted by the then second-in-command of the Regiment Major Alastair Morrison and SAS sergeant Barry Davies, the German anti-terrorist team successfully stormed the airliner, killing three out of the four Palestinian terrorists on board and freeing their terrified hostages.

Haley & Weller produce an entirely waterproof stun grenade which operates with a silent electrical fuse, allowing the thrower a good deal of discretion in its use. When the pin is pulled and the grenade is thrown, the fly-off lever remains in place, unlike other similar devices, and there is no initial report. Instead, a spring-loaded plunger is released allowing an electrical circuit to be closed. A tiny battery in the grenade's head then sends current to an electronic delay timer. When this delay time is complete an electric squib ignites the stun grenade. Variations of the original single loud report and flash effectively add to the surprise and cause even more shock to an adversary.

Mines

The extensive deployment of anti-personnel and anti-vehicle mines is taught to SAS recruits, and much time is spent learning their tactical use. Employing the right mine for each task, be it the faithful Claymore, or one of today's state-of-the-art 'smart-mines', can cause havoc to a large pursuing enemy force, and enables small SAS patrols to deny routes to an enemy in his own territory. Linked to a central control panel, several mines can be detonated in different areas at different times so, consequently, a large area can be monitored and explosions set off when the enemy intrudes into SAS-controlled space.

Missiles

Anti-tank weapons such as the LAW-80 which entered service in 1988, Milan, LAW-66 and the American Stinger anti-aircraft missile have been used by SAS operators since the Falklands War, though the latter two are by far the most preferred. The LAW-66 is a one-man-operated throwaway rocket launcher weighing only 1.36 kilos. Firing the 1 kilo rocket, which has a maximum range of 1,000 metres, a 66 carrying the M-18 warhead is capable of penetrating 305mm of armour. In practice, when fired at a stationary target a maximum effective range of 300 metres is more likely, and for moving targets, a practical distance of 150 metres is considered to be the maximum for a successful hit. When the 66 is fired, the rocket's motor is designed to burn all its propellant before the missile leaves the aluminium launcher, and six stabilizing fins then spring out to keep the missile straight and level in flight. The anti-tank M-18 warhead contains 340 grams of Octol, an incredibly potent high explosive which is capable of devastating the inside of tanks and other armoured vehicles.

The American Stinger anti-aircraft guided-missile system enables the infantryman to take on enemy aircraft in action and stand a very good chance of shooting them down despite counter-missile techniques taught to modern pilots. Developed by the US Army Missile Command, Stinger replaced the American Redeye anti-aircraft missile and is a 'fire and forget' weapon. Used to great effect by Mujaheddin guerrilla forces against the Soviets in the latter stages of the war in Afghanistan, Stinger is a shoulder-fired ground-to-air missile which carries a high explosive 'hit-to-kill' warhead and a dual-thrust rocket motor which separates from the main missile at a safe distance from the firer. To reduce an enemy aircraft's chances of surviving an attack by using electronic counter-measures and the technique of releasing 'chaff' to disorientate the missile, two or more Stingers are sometimes fired at the same target and at the same time. Built into the Stinger package is an 'identification-friend-or-foe' (IFF) interrogator enabling the user to confirm that his enemy is just that, rather than an aircraft from his own side.

Passive Night-Vision Devices

The concept that in order to win a firefight on the battlefield, the modern soldier requires weaponry that has just come off the designer's drawing board is contrary to SAS thinking, for an old rifle in the hands of an expert marksman can cause as much chaos as many modern weapons. Add to the rifle a night-vision capability and the weapon can become a nightmare to the enemy. For this reason much research has been carried out in recent years into the use and development of passive night-vision aids and thermal-imaging devices. Various defence systems manufacturers such as Thorn EMI and Pilkington Optronics have produced highly effective gun-mounted night-vision aids, though the tendency in SAS operations has been to use them only for observation of the enemy's movements. In close combat the soldier's own night vision is vital, and having to change constantly from normal vision to the distorted view he has through a PNV scope causes problems.

Early see-in-the-dark systems like the American Starlight Scope were heavy and cumbersome, and mounted on a rifle they were awkward to use effectively. US soldiers and marines who used them in Vietnam quickly realized, however, that this new tool in the hands of a marksman was a turning point in night combat, for now, instead of just firing illuminating parachutes flares, they could engage the enemy without being seen and the only thing that would give away their position was the muzzle flash of their own weapons.

Today's night sights have come a long way since they were first used in Vietnam, and Pilkington's Kite Sight for example is an extremely tough and lightweight weapon-aiming system that can be fitted to most combat rifles and anti-tank weapons, enabling the firer to engage an enemy in total darkness, while another, Maxi-Kite, is designed to fit sniper rifles. Variants of the Kite include binocular versions which can be used for short- and medium-range surveillance operations either held in the hand or face-mask mounted.

Perhaps the biggest advance in night-vision equipment is the introduction of thermal-image systems which are revolutionizing military and police operations. Any human or animal body which emits heat can now be seen from the ground or air, and the days when an enemy (or one's own forces) could successfully hide in a wood, buildings or long grass and escape under the cover of darkness are clearly numbered. However, as with all the latest technology someone is always considering how to create counter-measures, and the SAS as usual is in the forefront of such research.

Bergens and Belt-Kit
From the early days infantrymen struggled with the dilemma of how to carry their kit, which varied from mission to mission, and was inevitably awkward and heavy to carry. The SAS's solution to this problem was to invent a three-tiered system starting with the bergen. Initially this was the traditional tough canvas rucksack beloved by the early mountaineers, with a main

compartment for the sleeping-bag and clothing and, traditionally, two side pockets and a rear pocket for smaller items. Next was added 'belt-kit', which employed a number of canvas pouches for carrying water and ammunition, and the third 'layer' was the pockets of the soldier's clothing. A wide variety of versions were developed over the years, many belt-kits being hand- or machine-stitched by the men, who would adapt army-issued webbing themselves. At one time it was often possible to spot an SAS trooper in the field simply by looking at the fashion in which he wore his belt-kit, the pouches hanging lower on his waist belt than usual making it easier to carry a huge bergen, while some would wear as many as six or seven individual pouches.

Where a large number of pouches were worn, the soldier might add shoulder straps to support the weight of his ammunition and water bottles. The problem with canvas bergens and webbing was the weather, for when waterlogged by a heavy downpour or after crossing a river, they would almost double in weight, so military scientists eventually looked for a solution. In the 1970s a tough and waterproof material, butyl-laminate, was introduced into service and this started a revolution in kit-carrying equipment.

Chest rigs – pouches worn high on the body and held together with nylon netting[2] – appeared and were worn by men serving in Oman and elsewhere, and into these they placed more ammunition and hand grenades, but still these attempts at resolving the kit-carrying problem caused difficulties. Soldiers had learnt that fighting in full kit while wearing a bergen was not only exhausting but extremely dangerous as movement was impaired

[2] The netting idea came from an alert pair of eyes noticing the luggage rack in the compartment of a train, and ordering some of the mesh material.

and one's silhouette made it almost impossible to vanish into 'the soldier's best friend' (as retired SAS survival instructor Lofty Wiseman says), the hole in the ground.

Today's SAS trooper on 'Green Operations' (operations in camouflage combat fatigues) will normally wear his personally rigged low-slung belt-kit, now made of tough Cordura, with or without a yoke to support it. In this belt-kit he carries water bottles, ammunition and one pouch specially designed for survival equipment. Added to this he may add one of a number of styles of chest rigs for carrying extra ammunition, one of the most popular being a South African version. The trend towards chest webbing or combat-carrying-equipment-vests is a point of contention among some of the older hands who preferred the original and well-tried SAS belt-kit.

Needless to say, the debate still continues and strong opinions are voiced as to whether this or that item is 'magic kit'. The current SAS bergen which replaced the butyl-laminate version, also in Cordura, is made by the Barnstaple-based CQC company which produces the Web-90 system of kit-carrying equipment which is highly adaptable for today's modern soldier. Made in a choice of back sizes to fit soldiers of different heights, this is an excellent and highly adaptable rucksack with removable side pouches that can be zipped together to make a twin-compartment day sack, while a spacious roof comprises two enormous zipper compartments.

The Windproof

Traditionally, the item of clothing most prized by serving SAS personnel, apart from the sand-coloured beret, is 'the windproof', a tough cotton camouflaged smock with a hood and four spacious exterior pockets. Although the material is relatively thin, it is wind-resistant and quick-drying. Initially made from a close-weave Egyptian cotton, the smock, unlike some modern high-performance materials, is virtually silent when worn by a moving soldier. There is no tell-tale rustling noise when moving through vegetation, and the trousers, in matching material, feature six more large pockets. The standard-issue camouflaged disruptive pattern material (DPM) is infra-red resistant, and desert, snow and other camouflage patterns are available.

A recent variant of the SAS cotton smock is the ventile version whose properties were discovered by aircrew during the Second World War. An incredibly versatile and hardy fabric with the same advantages of silence as cotton, ventile was used by the RAF for aircrews' immersion suits, and is still used today for hospital surgeons' gowns. When the material becomes waterlogged the fibres swell, keeping water out and offering the wearer considerable protection. Though better at keeping out the elements than the cotton windproof, the ventile smock is really only rain resistant, and despite several worthy projects which prove beyond doubt its efficiency, SAS soldiers faced with days in soaking OPs will use Gore-Tex as an outer layer whenever possible. The remarkable qualities of this amazingly useful material have not been overlooked by the SAS and today the Regiment has a considerable quantity of it, including waterproof suits, bivvi-bags, gaiters, and even socks, and since Gore-Tex is both waterproof and breathable, the modern SAS trooper is able to stay dry (or reasonably so) for long periods in covert OPs or on the move.

Boots

Following some unpleasant experiences in the Falklands War, during which many soldiers suffered 'trench foot', a major project was initiated by the Ministry of Defence to create a fully waterproof combat boot. Some progress was made, and today's soldier is better equipped in the foot department than most of his predecessors, though research still continues. One solution for some SAS soldiers was to buy their own, and US Danner Arcadia boots with their built-in Gore-Tex shell became extremely popular, although the elevated price put many off them: 'Why, in the British Army' they asked 'should we have to buy ourselves a decent pair of boots?' Wearing non-issue kit of any kind is often frowned upon by the Headshed, though this of course does not restrict some of the more daring. In some ways it makes sense that all the soldiers in a patrol should be equipped identically not only for identification purposes, but also for re-supply.

If the group is cut off in some remote region for long periods and needs replacement kit, there is no time to order by high-speed morse 'A double-E fitting, size 10 Danner Arcadia please with a pair of zippets.' Standard operational procedure might just run to 'Send us No.345' – a pair of size 10 boots.

The reality for most of the men in the Regiment is making do with whatever boots are issued, lacing them up tight to give optimum support, and knowing how to keep the feet in good condition. No matter which boots are worn, be they stock standard-issue high-leg combats, desert boots, jungle boots or expensive Gore-Tex, unless the feet are used to trekking great distances blisters will form. Some expert walkers advise wearing a thin pair of socks under a thicker pair to reduce the friction-rub on the feet, and this technique, if you have a sufficient supply of socks in your pack, is certainly a good one. Other more drastic measures like soaking the feet in alcohol or coating them with a layer of Vaseline have been tried, but it is quite common to witness some of those who have just finished a long drag on the Brecon Beacons airing the heels and toes of their iodine-painted feet in the fresh air. As walking long distances is an intrinsic part of SAS soldiering, members pay special attention to their footwear, and are frequently seen off-duty in comfortable desert boots or good quality trainers.

Body Armour

For many years now, British armed forces have searched for lightweight but effective body armour. Most soldiers have always considered this to be a practical impossibility and have relied on their field skills to avoid being hit in a firefight. Today, however, with the improvement in bullet- and fragmentation-resistant materials, including ceramic plates capable of stopping high-velocity fire, the SAS soldier's wardrobe is changing. The CRW Pagoda team which stormed the Iranian Embassy in 1980 wore first-generation body armour, while their successors today have access to highly sophisticated and specialized body armour with integrated, secure communications systems.

The Armourshield GPV-25 vest has ceramic plates and a blunt-trauma shield front and back, and layered Kevlar around the body. Underneath this the Special Projects (SP) trooper wears a fire-retardant Nomex coverall which is designed to protect him from fire and flash burns. A specially made special forces helmet, the National Plastics AC100-1, built from layers of ballistic cloth, will protect the wearer from most small-arms fire, though the majority of SAS men have a natural aversion to wearing a helmet as they believe it restricts their all-round vision.

Each time a manufacturer comes up with a revolutionary armoured vest that he claims will stop this or that high-velocity round, Ops Research staff and some of the men who may ultimately wear it in combat take it to the range and blast it full of holes. More than one 'bullet-proof' vest has had to go back to the drawing board and start again before the SAS consider it any good.

Communications

Communications plays a vital role in the Regiment's operations and 264 Signals Regiment attached from the Royal Corps of Signals is dedicated to handling SAS transmissions and equipment. Based in Hereford, they are responsible for the day-to-day servicing and operation of radio and satellite communications from the standard MEL PRC-319 'burst-transmission' sets to the latest covert state-of-the-art concealable walkie-talkies. Since before the Falklands War SAS radio operators have been able to communicate directly with their command centre in Hereford thanks to a man-portable and easily erected satellite dish which reduces the delay in sending updated situation reports.

Encrypted morse, however, is still seen as the most rapid and reliable method of sending messages over long distances, and the use of digitized high-speed transmissions reduces the 'risk time' to the man on the ground from an enemy equipped with direction-finding equipment.

There is stiff competition between communications system manufacturers who are constantly improving the reliability and security of their products. Lightweight digital voice-encryption units like Racal Comsec's MA4470 and the MA4430 multi-function telephone units with a high-level encryption system offer secure 'comms' to the men in the field, while Racal's MA4477 can be fitted to normal patrol radios to uprate their security. Others like the Cougar 2000 have a totally secure FM and UHF system, and the hi-tech Panther 2000-V is currently the smallest and lightest 20-watt EPM radio in the world. The 2000-H is an 'intelligent' frequency-hopping radio transceiver, and not only has a low probability of intercept (LPI) but also incorporates an anti-jamming device. In the use of such sophisticated types of equipment, and others that are so secret they cannot be discussed here, the SAS and 264 Signals have a number of tricks to confuse anyone who succeeds in tracking and decoding their transmission frequencies. Just as behind-the-lines radio operators worked to a strict transmission timescale in the Second World War, today's elite forces will only send messages at pre-arranged times unless circumstances force them into using pre-planned emergency procedures.

Intruder Alarms

The success of special forces work depends strongly on the careful gathering of intelligence about an enemy, and then deciding how to use that information to its best advantage. A range of useful surveillance systems have emerged in recent times designed specifically to assist the soldier on the ground. The Shorrock 330 microwave fence is an intruder alarm system consisting of four or more small sensor units which can be set up in about half an hour and covers an area of 14,000 square metres. The range between transmitters and receivers is up to 120 metres and the invisible 'fence' is approximately 2.5 metres high. Anyone or anything crossing its perimeter signals an alarm, and the system functions in all conditions including rain and fog.

Racal's Classic RGS2740 remote ground-sensor system operates in a similar fashion and enables a soldier to plant up to eight sensors linked to a single receiver operated by the controller. The VHF signal received on the monitor is automatically decoded and the sensor's position and the type of intrusion is burst-transmitted to the display panel. Trip-wire and pressure-pad triggering systems can be incorporated, making the RGS2740 a highly adaptable and useful covert observation system.

Target Markers

Laser target markers (LTMs) which are used for pinpointing enemy positions and strategic targets have traditionally been cumbersome affairs unloved by fast-moving and lightly equipped special forces, but today's LTMs, like the Ferranti Type 306, have made targeting easier.

Operating in liaison with ground-attack aircraft like the RAF Tornado, Jaguar and Harrier, forward air controllers can guide aircraft into precision-bombing runs, thus reducing civilian casualties. A thermal imager can be added making the 306 effective in total darkness for covert night operations, and Ferranti's laser designator/ranger has the advantage of being one of the few man-portable systems on the market.

Navigation

Great advances have been made in navigation, and with the introduction of global positioning systems (GPS), which rely on twenty-four satellites circling the earth for their operation, a soldier is now able to locate his position on the map simply and accurately to within 10 metres by touching a few buttons on his pocket-sized Magellan navigator. Unlike the marine sextant, it is no longer necessary to take a 'fix' on the sun and use a chronometer to calculate longitude and latitude. Magellan does it all for you at any time of the day or night without the requirement of an advanced knowledge of mathematics or the solar system.

While extremely accurate (the Magellan can also work out time and distance calculations) few SAS troopers would exchange it for their trusty prismatic compass, which has been in service, virtually unchanged, for generations. With the weight of a small bomb, the prismatic has an extremely accurate sighting system enabling precise bearings to be taken on distant landmarks, and for resection, a method of locating your exact position by taking a bearing on at least two recognizable objects and plotting them on the map.

Unlike the civilian hill walker's compass, soldiers' compasses are calibrated in mils and not degrees (6,400 mils equals 360 degrees), making them extremely accurate, especially for artillery control. The modern featherlight Silva and Suunto plastic protractor compasses used by orienteering enthusiasts are popular for their simplicity, though in battle conditions some soldiers say they have a tendency to break. Having said that, many a special forces soldier wears one fixed to the breast-pocket buttonhole of his windproof.

Knives

The choice of knife carried by SAS men depends to a great extent on the mission they are involved in, but in general, most will carry a small folding one that locks open. The wide range of multi-bladed knives has its uses and is excellent for a variety of tasks, but under extreme conditions they may not be sufficiently hardy. Great attention is paid to the manner in which a knife is kept sharp, and state-of-the-art sharpening kits are popular. The Malayan parang, Gurkha kukri and the machete are often carried for serious backwoods work and are ideal for shelter building and chopping firewood.

The famous Fairbairn Sykes commando dagger once issued to many of Britain's special forces is hardly ever seen in the hands of an SAS trooper despite the mythology that goes with that dagger. One hardened veteran of the Regiment's operations said, 'Why use a dagger? If it's for killing someone, you're much better off with a butcher's knife. They're cutting up meat all day long and it works all right for them, doesn't it?' Another retired SAS man, the charismatic John 'Lofty' Wiseman, for many years the Regiment's top survival instructor, went into business a few years ago and designed an excellent parang-style knife which can be used like a machete, and because of its clever design, it is also ideal for more delicate work such as gutting fish.

Close-Combat Shooting
From his first day as a member of the Regiment, the SAS soldier is trained exhaustively in the techniques of close-combat pistol shooting until he reaches an extra-ordinary level of skill. The old 'double-tap' technique of hitting the target accurately with groups of two rounds is still practised by some enthusiasts, but in a close-combat situation an SAS trooper is taught to fire fast and accu-rately at his target until it ceases to be a threat. In an urban firefight, for example in Northern Ireland, or dur-ing the Gibraltar shootings, an SAS man who decides to fire will have been trained to kill his adversary and not wound. Consequently, once the decision to engage the target has been made, he will usually keep firing until his victim shows no visible sign of threat. His rate of fire will probably astonish pistol manufacturers, for the speed described in published data for SAS handguns of 40 rounds per minute is greatly surpassed by constant prac-tice on the range. During siege-training scenarios at the 'Killing House' in Hereford, it is not unusual for a troop-er to fire a full 13-round magazine from a Browning Hi-Power in less than 3 seconds. The operation of drawing the pistol from the holster is usually accomplished in under a second, and magazine changes, when carried out by experienced hands, remind an observer of a fast gear

change in a car; when it is skilfully done there is virtually no break in the course of fire. Both the Browning Hi-Power and the newer Sig Sauer weapons have an effective range of about 45 metres, and in the hands of an experienced SAS soldier they will be effective at such distances. As anyone who is familiar with such weapons knows, the problem with a 'semi', as gun enthusiasts call them, is the annoying tendency they sometimes have of jamming. A stoppage in a combat situation can cost a soldier his life, so intensive training is given to the SAS trooper enabling him to clear such hazards rapidly. Furthermore, by selecting good quality factory-loaded ammunition for their firearms and maintaining their handguns in exceptional condition, such occurrences are kept to a minimum. Above all, the Regiment's soldiers are required to 'Train, train and train again' until their marksmanship with aimed shots and their 'sense-of-direction' shooting becomes second nature.

'Big Brother Is Watching You'

Perhaps the single biggest technical advance in the fight against armed terrorists is the ability to watch them without them knowing. The advances in miniature cameras and thermal-imaging systems during the last ten years have totally changed the style of such covert operations. Today it is possible to hide a miniature video-surveillance camera anywhere the operator chooses from a derelict house in a built-up area to the corner of a field. Such covert operations nearly always result from the careful gathering of intelligence, for there is no point in wasting hours of valuable security force's time watching a farmhouse when the terrorists are miles away in a pub.

The 'eye in the sky' helicopter-mounted surveillance camera can respond rapidly to reports of terrorist activity in a particular area, and using infrared cameras or thermal-imaging systems, the latter locating body heat, it is possible to find a hidden gunman in thick undergrowth or dense forest in daylight, fog or total darkness (see 'Passive Night-Vision Devices' in this chapter, p. 76). Not only can a living human being be spotted from the air at night, but where he has just been in the preceding minutes can also be identified, and this applies also to corpses.

Of course, such systems do have their limitations. Helicopter operations can sometimes be restricted by weather conditions, and the noise of the machine's rotors can usually be heard over great distances. Despite these minor drawbacks, the traditional hiding places for those who are running from the law are no longer safe, and helicopters using GPS can now pass exact coordinates to follow-up ground forces to guide them to their targets. From a distance of 3,000 metres helicopters can read the registration number of a moving vehicle and follow it for hours until roadblocks or chase vehicles are deployed to catch it. The only real restrictions to such operations are financial and moral. Do we want strangers watching us as we mow the lawn or walk the dog at midnight? The strongest argument in favour of 'eyes in the sky', which is the same as that employed in the debate about British citizens carrying identity cards, is that unless you are up to no good you have nothing to fear from the forces of law and order.

Whether we like it or not, in Northern Ireland for many years, and today on the mainland of Great Britain, the helicopters are watching us, although for most of the time we are unaware of their presence. Television 'police' programmes showing the drama of high-speed car chases and villains being chased across fields at night are clearly making lawbreakers think twice about their criminal *modus operandi*, and as long as the political will is there, the taxpayer agrees, and civil liberties groups fail to stop them, airborne watchers look like becoming a permanent fixture in our skies.

As with every military-use technological development, counter-measures are developed to neutralize them, and there is no doubt that the SAS are today capable of beating thermal-imaging and infrared systems.

FIVE

OPERATION 'NIMROD' – THE IRANIAN EMBASSY

You close in on the target, you don't stand back. You hear people say you've got to win the firefight . . . that's bullshit! You're not going in there to have a firefight. A firefight is when someone is shooting at you and you're shooting back. You're not going in there to let these guys shoot at you. There's only one side shooting and that's you and your team so what you do is you close in, it's body language. Every time I take a pace forward my shooting gets easier. I know what I'm going to do and by the time I get there I'm going to show you . . . if I haven't shot you already. It's absolutely psychological. That's why they originally came up with the black gas mask because of the psychological effect of having this sinister alien-type person closing in on you.

(SP Team member)

At 11:32 on the morning of 30 April 1980, six members of a terrorist group calling themselves 'Mujaheddin Anafar Martyr'[1] forced their way into the Iranian Embassy at 16

[1] The Group of the Martyr. In 680 AD the ruling Caliph of Damascus faced a rebellion by a young man named Hassan whose father had

Prince's Gate, Kensington, London and took the twenty-six occupants hostage. As well as the sixteen members of the embassy's staff there were Iranian, Pakistani and British nationals including two BBC employees in the building that day, and Police Constable Trevor Lock, an armed member of the Diplomatic Protection Group. The embassy's alarm system, connected with New Scotland Yard, operated at 11:36 and armed DPG officers were deployed to secure the area around the embassy.

By 11:31 the embassy area was contained by two armed police sergeants and seven constables forming what was to become the inner cordon of the most dramatic and violent anti-terrorist operation ever seen on British soil.

At 12:09 police established contact with the gunmen, and two control centres, Alpha Control (forward control point) and Zulu Control (base station) were set up. Movement in front of Prince's Gate was restricted unless hidden from the embassy's windows, and a high brick wall at the front of the premises was put to good use protecting the movement of officers across the front of the stronghold. The area at the rear, a communal garden for Prince's Gate properties, provided plenty of cover for a watch on the rear windows, while nearby flats made ideal sniper positions and excellent observation points. What Oan, the leader of the terrorist group did not know was that the Metropolitan Police, and more significantly the SAS, had been waiting for such an event as this to happen. A former member of the SAS's

been murdered by the Caliph's soldiers. During the ensuing battle Hassan was killed. Shia Muslims still mourn his death to this day and claim him as a martyr to their cause. Thirteen hundred years later, Oan, Makki, Faisal, Ali, Hassan and Shai calling themselves Mujaheddin Anafar Martyr attacked the Iranian Embassy in London 'in the cause of Arabistan'.

D Squadron, Dusty Gray, then a police dog handler, heard about the events at the embassy and phoned the Regiment's headquarters. By three o'clock that afternoon an advanced party of SAS men were at the scene.

At the Killing House in Hereford early that Wednesday morning it was business as usual, and for the members of the SP team on stand-by it looked like being another routine day on the firing range. Then suddenly, at 11:48 the SP Team's bleeper began sounding and Operation 'Nimrod' had begun. Instead of heading for the SAS's London base, the Duke of York's Barracks in Chelsea, the planners decided that in view of the large media interest in the siege story it would be wiser to hide the SP Team in the barracks at Regent's Park, and it was there late on Wednesday night that the first of the Regiment's Range Rovers began arriving.

Gaining intelligence by technical means was a high priority, and because of the need to isolate the terrorists from the outside world, telephone wires and television aerial cables were cut. By the end of the first day the police Operations Support Group (C7) had installed video-surveillance cameras to maintain a continuous watch on the embassy building. The same day at 4:20 pm the embassy Third Secretary, twenty-six-year-old Frieda Mozafarian, was released, and then on Thursday, 1 May at 11:20 am, Chris Cramer one of the BBC employees who had been at the embassy with colleague Sim Harris to apply for visas, was also released, suffering from acute stomach pains. This was the break the police and the SAS planners had been hoping for. In the hands of an experienced interrogator and under the right conditions, invaluable detail can be gleaned from an eye-witness. Now they had one who spoke clear English, and the men who might have to risk their lives inside the Iranian Embassy were going to make the most of him.

By now the cordons around the building were well established and preparations for a long wait were in hand. A box on a pole proved to be a simple but effective way of passing objects into the building, and this rather cunning technique also served for gathering the fingerprints of some of those inside. Food was provided by the police catering branch and when this was collected at the front door, Anti-Terrorist Squad (C13) officers took the opportunity of photographing its collection with telephoto lenses. As the hours went by, more and more information was being amassed by the siege-breakers, and a police negotiating team led by the skilful Superintendent Fred Luff and backed up by Commander Peter Duffy, head of C13, negotiated through an interpreter with the terrorist leader, Oan.

For the SP Team members of B Squadron, who were divided into Red and Blue teams, the routine of waiting for something to happen was not unusual. Each time B Squadron had been on SP duties in the past they had rehearsed scenarios exactly like this. Sometimes the target had been a remote mansion or a commercial airliner far away from the public's view, and on other occasions British Rail would close a station on a Sunday morning, using the cover of a 'major incident', so that the Regiment could rehearse a hostage-rescue operation, but such exercises did not ease their boredom. At Regent's Park barracks carpenters using plans of the embassy were hurriedly building a scale model, while SAS planners examined the options available to them for a forced entry into the building.

The forty-eight-strong SAS team consisting of NCOs, corporals and troopers, with a captain leading each of the two assault groups, was commanded by the no-nonsense Major Hector Gullan. On secondment from the Parachute Regiment, and nicknamed 'Hector the Protector', Gullan, with his cool and methodical mind, set about planning the 'neutralization' of Mujaheddin Anafar Martyr. Oan and his group of misguided terrorists had not counted on Hector. If they had, they would probably have stayed in Arabistan.

So why were they there? In the years following their London 'adventure', Oan and his companions were discovered to have been in London on a mission conceived in Baghdad by Iraqi Intelligence. Unknown to Oan, the group's chances of survival were extremely uncertain. One of the gunmen, Sami Mohammed Ali, was travelling on what Iraqi authorities claimed was an authorized diplomatic passport, and all of the group when filling in their visa applications had stated that they were coming to the United Kingdom for medical treatment. They had been told by their Iraqi Intelligence handler that this operation was to be a rapid affair, that their task was to draw the attention of Western powers to the plight of Arabs living under the tyrannical Ayatollah Ruhollah Khomeini in Iran, and that they would return home as heroes within a few days.

Equipping the terrorist team with weapons and grenades was achieved easily by Ali with his diplomatic immunity and the use of the Iraqi Embassy's diplomatic bag without the Embassy's knowledge, and as they prepared their operation, the terrorists were encouraged by news of the disastrous events at Desert One.[2] It seemed to Oan, Ali and the other members of the group that the West was hopelessly impotent in dealing with terrorists.

The commanding officer of 22 SAS in 1980 was Lieutenant-Colonel Michael Rose, and his immediate superior,

[2] In April 1980 a covert operation to release American hostages in Tehran, Iran, failed when US helicopters carrying members of Delta Force crashed at a refuelling point, Desert One, in the Iranian desert leaving eight dead.

Brigadier Peter de la Billière, was the Director of the United Kingdom's Special Forces. As events unfolded at the Iranian Embassy de la Billière briefed Prime Minister Margaret Thatcher and her Cabinet and presented them with an SAS solution to the drama. It would be feasible, he told Thatcher, to achieve a successful military conclusion to the hostage-taking at the embassy with minimum loss of life, adding that if possible such an operation should be carried out in daylight. The rescuers were already in place and an assault plan had reached an advanced state of preparation. Mrs Thatcher made it clear to de la Billière that she would never make deals with terrorists and that if Oan and his men could not be persuaded to give themselves up and there was loss of life, a military solution would be employed.

De la Billière had already worked out how he and the SAS would end the siege. The fine detail had not yet been worked out, but he knew that with the calibre of men he could call on in the Regiment's Special Projects teams, sorting out a handful of Arab terrorists would not be a great problem. If there were to be losses to his raiding force or among the hostages, then there would certainly be political repercussions. With this in mind he called together the men who were at the sharp end of the operation, Mike Rose and Hector Gullan. De la Billière's wife Bridget cooked spaghetti that evening and as they ate, the three men examined the options. Rose had thoroughly investigated the layout of the embassy building and its gardens and had found an excellent holding area for the SP Team, which was on stand-by. Next door to 16 Prince's Gate was the Royal College of General Practitioners which occupied numbers 14 and 15. Rose had wasted no time in immediately smuggling twenty-four men led by an officer (Red Team) inside. The initial plan, prepared on the first day, was for Rose's men to break into the embassy at the top floor and using copious amounts of CS gas, fight their way downwards in the hope of saving at least some of the hostages.

However, given time – the more the better – the three men concluded that if the building could be stormed from a number of points at the same time and diversions were created to put the terrorists off guard, casualties should, in theory, at least, be relatively light. Such a plan would most certainly achieve all the aims of the operation, and reduce the risk of political flak from Whitehall. Most importantly of all, the losses of SAS personnel would be kept to a minimum.

Next door to the terrorists' stronghold, on the other side at number 17, was the Ethiopian Embassy. After careful negotiations and at the risk of causing a diplomatic incident, the Ethiopians agreed to let the SAS in. Intelligence on what was happening inside number 16 was now of vital importance, and having arranged for the local gas board to create a good deal of noise in the street outside the building, ostensibly repairing a gas main, SAS men and surveillance experts from MI5 began drilling the walls adjoining the Iranian Embassy in order to plant microphones and fibre-optic spy cameras. Unfortunately the walls, they quickly discovered, were almost two feet thick, and the amount of noise made by the gas men outside which was required to drown the banging and drilling inside soon brought suspicion and complaints from the terrorists. Mike Rose suggested that aircraft approaching Heathrow airport might be persuaded to descend to a low altitude, thus adding to the general din in the area. Amazingly this was agreed, and shortly after the request was made, aircraft were roaring overhead at low level.

At half-past three on the morning of the third day, Blue Team managed to reach the Royal College of

General Practitioners building without being noticed by either the terrorists or the press. This had now been designated the forward holding area, and Red Team, which had been on stand-by in the building since the start of the siege, was finally relieved. They returned to Regent's Park for some sleep and a decent meal.

Inside the embassy the strain was beginning to show on the hostages, and that meant in all likelihood it was badly affecting the terrorists as well. Gradually the demands from Oan[3] the terrorist's leader started to alter; now, instead of demanding the release of prisoners in Iran, he began asking for a coach to take him and the hostages to an airport. Now he wanted an aircraft to take him and the hostages to the Middle East.

Without realizing it, BBC man Chris Cramer had indirectly given Hector Gullan and his men valuable information about Oan's group. A stickler for fine detail, Gullan had been able to discover from several sources including observations made by Cramer that there were six terrorists in the embassy building, not five as first believed, and that their armoury consisted of two Polish-origin WZ-63 (PM63) machine pistols, which fire a 9mm ¥ 18 cartridge and use 25- or 40-round magazines. Similar to the Soviet-bloc Skorpion, this weapon was designed to fire single shots one-handed, and for fully automatic firing, a collapsible shoulder-stock and front handgrip are fitted. Oan's group also had between them one Spanish .38 revolver and three Browning 9mm pistols, similar to the one Gullan himself carried. Added to this arsenal were a number of Soviet RGD-5 anti-personnel fragmentation grenades which in the open have a killing range of up to 20 metres – in the confines of one of the embassy's rooms these would be

[3] Oan Ali Mohammed called himself Salim in negotiations with police.

lethal if they were used. The unknown factor facing the rescuers was that as well as these weapons, there was the possibility that Oan's men had rigged the building with explosives, and if that were the case, the loss of life during such a rescue would inevitably be high, perhaps unjustifiably so. One of the men who served in the SP Team described the practice behind the theory of siege-breaking:

All of a sudden somebody comes in wearing all this gear [counter-revolutionary warfare kit] . . . Jesus! They come in, they close the distance down and make their shooting easier. Their body language is, 'I'm coming for you.' I'm not alone, there's another guy behind me, so there's two, perhaps three guys coming in here. They might peel off but I'm getting impatient now saying what are you going to do? I know what I am going to do. Every pace I get closer, my confidence is getting bigger. You've now got two seconds at the most to make the most fantastic decision of your life. Who's in control? It doesn't matter what *you* do, *I* am in control. Well fine, do you want to make a shooting of this? You are dead. You've got the total advantage because you know what you're going to do, when you're going to do it and how you're going to do it and you're not alone regardless of the fact that people may know when it is going to happen. To me it's two elements of surprise, the initial element and the second. The back door goes BANG! What the hell was that? As long as you keep the momentum and the aggression going you always have the secondary element. I teach S.A.S., Surprise, Aggression and Speed. Any two of those three will always make the third. If you've got a good element of surprise and a good speed then you've got the aggression. If you've the aggression and speed . . . and so on. It will always feed off each other. The one that gets abused is speed. Again, it's that body language. Somebody that's coming towards you obviously gives the body language that they are confident and they're going to do whatever they say they're going to do. Somebody that stops and makes a verbal comment, well, their body language suggests they're not really happy about the circumstances. Now the contradiction to that is what sort of operations is the SAS going to be called in on versus that of a police operation. Technically, when the SAS are called in it means that nobody else at that stage can do the job, like the Iranian Embassy. There have been people that have been killed, hostages have been killed. It's escalating beyond all control and the only way this thing is going to be finished is to send an armed, aggressive team in. So you can get away doing slightly different tactics because the overall reason that you're going in is going to be a lot different to that of a law enforcement agency. In law enforcement 99 per cent of the time you're going in to arrest somebody, not necessarily to go in and shoot. So you're going in there as a team and the best way you can arrest somebody is to get within arm's reach, so again, movement. Counter-terrorism-wise you're expecting some sort of heavy action. You're expecting to be shot at. You're expecting, as in the Iranian Embassy, explosives in the building and they may have grenades. It's more orchestrated, it's basic military room combat. It is like an infantry battalion taking out a village . . . they've got to go into the house to take it out.

While the world's press cameramen peered through telephoto lenses at the embassy's windows and journalists searched for interesting detail to liven up their stories, an occasional jogger dressed in running kit could be seen sprinting across Hyde Park in the sunshine, but few of the reporters paid this any attention. One of the runners in the park was a B Squadron sergeant from Fiji who had survived the Battle of Mirbat in 1972, and at that time was the most highly decorated soldier in the British Army. Jogging around Hyde Park was an excellent way of releasing the tension that SAS troopers were under during those waiting days, and it also kept them in peak condition for what some of them were beginning to realize might be a very dangerous mission. Each day there were updated briefings on the current situation inside the embassy and by using fibre-optic cameras and listening devices more and more detail was becoming available about the hostages and the terrorists.

Members of Blue and Red Teams took it in turns to be available for immediate action in the event that they were required and for hours they sat around on the roof in full CRW kit keeping low to avoid camera lenses, weapons loaded and ready to go. The embassy's caretaker had by now been found and he was able to describe in fine detail the interior of the building with the aid of the rapidly built plywood scale model. Information that the windows of 16 Prince's Gate were armoured[4] and that the front door was reinforced, led to a rapid change of SAS plans. Initially they had thought that a few sledgehammers would be sufficient for gaining entry, but now they would have to use explosives.

Movement to and from the embassy was achieved by the stealth and cunning for which the SAS is notorious. As much as possible this was done under the cover of darkness, but where soldiers were obliged to move by vehicle, they used a pair of red Ford Transit vans, specially rented from Avis, leaving their Range Rovers at the Regent's Park barracks. During one of their midnight

[4] During the Shah of Iran's reign the SAS had advised the Iranians to install armoured glass.

vigils on the roof SAS men succeeded in opening the embassy skylight which had been left unlocked. In the moonlight they could just make out that this led into a top-floor bathroom. They had found an unguarded entry point. The temptation to dive straight in and engage the terrorists was enormous, but resigning themselves to the fact that thay had no orders to act, they returned to their holding point to report the discovery.

At 9:00 pm on Saturday the BBC broadcast the gunmen's demands in full, and in return a Pakistani tourist, Ali Ghanzafar was released. By the fifth day, Sunday, 4 May, five hostages had been released by dint of careful negotiations, all of them for medical reasons, but the terrorists' demands that political prisoners in Iran be freed had fallen on deaf ears in Tehran. In Whitehall, Foreign Office officials held urgent meetings with Syrian, Jordanian, Algerian and Kuwaiti diplomats in an attempt to glean more information about the terrorist group, and also to make it abundantly clear that the British government could not give in to threats. Saddam Hussein, the Iraqi President, had badly misjudged Britain's mood. There was no way that Oan and his men were going to walk out of the Iranian Embassy, board a flight to freedom and receive a heroes' welcome in any Arab state.

Attempts to resolve the siege by peaceful means took a turn for the worse the following day when at 1:31 pm shots were heard from inside the embassy. Frustrated by the lack of progress that had been made, Oan decided to raise the stakes and show that unless he and his group were allowed to leave with their hostages for an unidentified destination, he was quite prepared to kill them all. All afternoon the negotiating team tried to ascertain exactly what was going on inside the embassy, and finally at 6:50 pm there were more shots and the body of Iranian press attaché Abbas Lavasani, who had been murdered in the embassy's basement,[5] was dumped outside the front door.

As the tension mounted the Home Secretary, William Whitelaw, met senior Foreign Office officials and told them that Prime Minister Margaret Thatcher was determined to deal the terrorists a blow that would be heard around the world. Oan made it clear to negotiators by telephone that he insisted on seeing the Arab ambassadors the British government had been talking to at the Foreign Office, and that unless this happened immediately he would execute another hostage.

Deputy Assistant Commissioner (Operations) John Dellow recalls the tension:

> We tried to continue with the strategy that I had employed throughout the six days. Negotiation is largely a matter of trying to get something out of somebody else after giving something. We were realizing that we were coming towards the end of what could be offered reasonably, knowing the government's attitude to terrorism and there was a clear indication that we were going to have very difficult negotiations. Negotiators work extremely hard to keep a dialogue going. All the time [a dialogue was taking place] we felt that hostages were not being shot. We tried to impress on the terrorists exactly what would happen in this country as opposed to other parts of the world, that if they didn't harm anybody they would come out unharmed themselves. That didn't make much of an impression and gradually as the day wore on things were becoming a little unstable and fractious inside the Iranian Embassy, and it became apparent after a time that we were not going to get very far with the normal sort of negotiations that we had had in the past.

[5] Lavasani had in fact been killed earlier that day.

It would be about this time that threats became apparent of shooting hostages. Eventually some shots were heard. The first around midday. It's difficult to judge whether in fact that was a bluff or not. It's quite a decision to make at that stage, we had to look at a lot of evidence. We began to believe that the chances of it being a bluff were lesser rather than greater, and shots were heard again later on. A body was eventually put out. It was my opinion that we could not risk the threat then being made of a succession of hostages being shot. It was at this stage that I advised the [Police] Commissioner that the matter should be resolved by military assault. This was passed on to government and the Home Secretary who gave his authority, and we finished the siege.

At 7:20 pm that Bank Holiday Monday, the members of Red Team were in position on the roof of 16 Prince's Gate and looping abseiling ropes through figure-of-eight descendeurs clipped to their climbing harnesses. Their responsibility would be the upper two floors, while Blue Team, ready at the rear in the embassy's garden, would tackle the basement, ground and first floors. Other Pagoda Team members would enter through the skylight on the roof. All they were waiting for now were three key words.

Speaking to Oan (who was still employing his *nom de guerre* 'Salim') on a field telephone which had been set up in the embassy, the police negotiator had the unenviable and difficult task of distracting the terrorists in order to prevent them from seeing SAS activity on the roof of the building.

Negotiator: Mr Trevor will only be able to drive one coach, won't he?

Salim: One is enough. About twenty-five seats . . . twenty-nine seats, sorry.

Negotiator: Now, whereabouts shall we put that coach first?

Salim: Opposite the door.

Negotiator: Well, opposite the door is a very vague phrase. If you're looking out of the window . . .

Salim: After we've checked it, then you will put it beside the door.

Negotiator: Well, let's talk about that then.

Salim: Okay.

Negotiator: Opposite the front door, you're looking straight out over the park . . .

Salim: And after we've checked it you will . . .

Negotiator: Yeah, can you listen to me and we'll just talk about the first movement of the coach up to the front door. Now, if you look out of the window directly ahead of you is the park. Now, to the right there is just the end of the wall and that is where those gas men were working on the generators . . . they were working on the gas leak.

Salim: Okay, I'll phone you after a few minutes . . . I go, I'll come again.

Negotiator: No, let's talk about this Salim.

Salim: No, they're asking [for] me . . . just a few minutes, I'll go, I'll come again.

Negotiator: Hallo Salim? Salim?

Salim: You know we are listening to some suspicious movement.

As they spoke, Red Team members were abseiling down to their targets while Blue Team were preparing to blast their way in through the rear at ground level.

Negotiator: Salim, there is no suspicious movement.

> *Salim:* Okay, just a minute, I'll come back ... I'm going
> to check.
>
> *Negotiator:* Salim ... Salim? There is no suspicious
> movement ...

At 7:23 pm a television reporter described seeing two figures 'dressed like frogmen' climbing on to a balcony at the front of 16 Prince's Gate from the adjoining number 15. Their frame-charge of C-4 plastic explosive, constructed specially to blow out the armoured windows on the first floor, exploded with a blinding flash and rocked the front of the building, while a second charge lowered from the roof was detonated inside the stairwell. Another, designed to shatter the reinforced french windows at the rear ground floor could not be used as the Red Team's lead abseiler descending the rear wall had become entangled in his rope. As he tried to release himself, his comrades used sledgehammers to smash their way in. Through the earphones under their anti-flash hoods came the order 'GO! GO! GO!'

What goes through the mind of a trooper as he storms through the window of a building held by terrorists?

Once you're going through the door you're in code red, your mind is a hundred per cent alert. Time slows down and you feel like the six-million-dollar man where you're trying to pick up 85 million pieces of information in a fraction of a second. Eyes going everywhere. Your whole body is exploding into speed and you're ready for all kinds of encounters. One of the things about room combat in house assaults is that you're always conscious about turning that corner, going through the next door, entering that room, so the very aspect of doing room combat keeps you at this high level. It's very rare that someone is shocked. What you do is you go back to surprise, aggression and speed.

> You're taking that straight to the person [the terrorist]
> instead of hoping that you may put down the odd round
> and perhaps hit the guy.
>
> (SP Team member)

From strategic points around the building SAS snipers
scanned the embassy's windows looking for targets of
opportunity, and fired CS gas so as to disorientate the
terrorists further. By now, all except one of the latter
were facing imminent death. Once the decision to send
in the SAS had been taken there was little chance of the
terrorists leaving the building alive, for the simple reason that as long as they were living and had their
weapons they represented a threat to the hostages and
the assault team.

Critics of the final violent solution approved by Margaret Thatcher have argued that it would have been possible to shout a warning such as 'Lay down your arms
and come out with your hands up.' Ask any SAS trooper about that and he will shake his head in disbelief, for
too many soldiers and policemen have been killed in
just those circumstances.

For some who served in the SP Team the days leading up to the assault were, in some ways, like training:

> The difference between a training exercise and the Iran-
> ian Embassy is that firstly it went on for longer, training
> exercises usually only last twenty-four hours or so,
> sometimes two days. The other difference was the
> exhaustion, constant stand-downs, waiting for some-
> thing to happen, have a draining effect on the metabo-
> lism, but really as far as room combat is concerned the
> only difference was that this time we had live targets. It's
> that motion . . . and absolute horror on people's faces.
> You completely take away their options. You get on to
> that person so fast they really cannot make a decision

for themselves. You, as the assault team member going in are making those decisions for them. You have to remember that the average person in the Regiment is around twenty-seven or twenty-eight so you don't have a green recruit. Most of them have been at platoon sergeant level, they've been in positions of authority. They've been promoted because of professionalism and reliability. You then have a very hard selection, so that means that people who get into the SAS want to be there. You have guys from all the services, so that brings a vast amount of other experience, and they're willing to go a little bit further than the average person.

In the eleven minutes that followed, the SAS shot dead five of the six terrorists with cool efficiency (one was hit eighty-two times) and nineteen hostages were released unharmed. One hostage, Ali Samed Zadeh was shot dead by a terrorist as the SP Team stormed in, and two others, including the embassy's medical adviser were wounded. One of the troopers recalled having 'a fearsome rush of adrenalin' as he heard the order to attack and broke in through the back of the building, and how the weight of his heavy body armour with its ceramic high-velocity plates 'felt like a T-shirt'.

Thankfully for the SP Team, rumours that Oan and his men had booby-trapped the building with explosives proved to be unfounded, and as the terrorists were cut down one by one, the task of getting the hostages out of the building became an urgent priority.

Some of the stun grenades had started fires inside the embassy's rooms and within minutes the building was ablaze. Hostages, their eyes streaming from the effects of tear gas, were bundled down the main staircase, thrown bodily from one SAS man to another until they were all safely on the grass in the garden. Each was unceremoniously laid face down, their hands tied with white plasticuffs while they were thoroughly searched. With them the SAS found Makki Hounoun Ali, a twenty-five-year-old member of the gang who had managed to hide amongst the hostages. Then, quite unexpectedly, some of the B Squadron men found themselves in the company of a beaming William Whitelaw, the Home Secretary, who had turned up at the scene to witness for himself how events were unfolding. According to one soldier, 'old Oyster-Eyes' had tears of joy unashamedly running down his cheeks.[6]

By 8:30 pm the siege-breakers had cleared the embassy building and having climbed out of their assault kit were piling into the red Avis vans at the front of the adjoining building, number 14. Escorted by a posse of police motorcycle outriders, the convoy raced away from the scene and headed back to the Regent's Park barracks. There, a large quantity of Foster's lager was awaiting them – and so too was Prime Minister Margaret Thatcher. As they settled down to watch the 10 o'clock news on television, somebody with a thick Glasgow accent abruptly shouted at her to 'Sit down!' as he could not see the screen. The Prime Minister, looking over her shoulder, obeyed the order without a word.

[6] At the outbreak of the Second World War, William Whitelaw had served in the Scots Guards with David Stirling (see Chapter One).

SIX

ACROSS THE WATER - NORTHERN IRELAND

'Tell me, Major,' asked Prime Minister Thatcher, 'how long do you think it will take you to defeat the IRA?' The dark-haired SAS officer considered the question carefully. This was not just another stuffed shirt from Whitehall but the nation's leader. They were all the same these politicians. He thought back to his happy childhood in the Chimanimani mountains of Rhodesia before sanctions forced that country to its knees, and to the SAS men from C Squadron who had died fighting against Robert Mugabe's and Joshua Nkomo's guerrillas. Fixing Mrs Thatcher with a look straight between the eyes, he replied sardonically, and with the hint of a smile, 'How long, ma'am, is a piece of string?' The task would not be quick or easy, and this was not a war that could be won by soldiers alone without an unflinching political commitment.

In 1922 the electorate in the newly created independent state of Eire voted its acceptance of Britain's partition of Ireland, democratically separating the twenty-six counties in the south, from Ulster,[1] the six counties in the north, which remain today under British

[1] Ulster before partition originally comprised nine counties, three of which joined Eire

rule. Many Republicans in the south considered this arrangement to be a sell-out on the part of the newly elected Dublin government. The Irish Republican Brotherhood, a secret society which had opposed Britain's presence in Ireland for more than a hundred years, had been succeeded in 1916 during the Easter Rebellion in Dublin by the newly formed Irish Republican Army. The IRA demanded nothing less than a total British withdrawal and a completely united Ireland. In the north two years later, soldiers of the British Army, who before the war had been dedicated to the principle that Ulster should remain part of the United Kingdom, returned from the carnage of the First World War. They landed, bloodied and scarred, to a heroes' welcome in predominantly Protestant Ulster.

In August 1969, during the first weeks of the current 'Troubles'[2] in Northern Ireland, Labour Prime Minister Harold Wilson sent the British Army on to the streets of Belfast and Londonderry to support the Royal Ulster Constabulary (RUC) in keeping the peace. With them were members of 22 Special Air Service Regiment who had a special role to play. The UVF, disbanded after the First World War, had re-formed as a terrorist organization, and were now the armed wing of the Ulster Defence Association, the UDA. In the rising tension of the times the UVF were suspected by British Intelligence of trying to organize the smuggling of arms shipments into the Antrim coast to counter the threat from the newly formed Provisional IRA (PIRA or 'Provos'). The PIRA (whose members were mostly of Catholic origin) which had broken away from the original, Official IRA (the

[2] During their first tour in Ulster from September to November 1969, D Squadron were based at Newtownards, the home of one of the 'Originals', Paddy Mayne. Wearing their best 'number ones' (uniforms), they laid a wreath at his grave.

'Stickies') during a heated argument about tactics in Dublin in December 1969, believed solely in an armed struggle against the 'British occupation of Ireland', while Protestant 'Loyalist' gunmen of the UVF were determined to stop them. UVF men like Gusty Spence had a strong following amongst the more extremist elements in Protestant areas of the province, and Wilson's government saw the very real threat of civil war breaking out.

Following the disbandment of the B Specials, the infamous – and often brutal – paramilitary volunteer RUC force which had antagonized the Catholic population for so many years, there was a real danger that the embittered former members of that force would pledge their allegiance to men like Spence. Allegations of brutality and even summary execution by the 'B-men' in the province, and comparisons with the activities of the Black and Tans (the auxiliary division of the Royal Irish Constabulary, raised during the original Troubles in Ireland of 1919–21) before Irish partition, led to the setting up of the Scarman Tribunal.

Lord Scarman investigated, amongst other incidents, the death of eight-year-old Patrick Rooney who was murdered at his home in the Catholic Lower Falls Road in Belfast when the B Special crew of a Shorland armoured car indiscriminately opened fire with their Browning heavy machine gun. Since the birth of the civil rights movement in Northern Ireland, and a total breakdown of law and order on its streets, the province was heading for disaster. This was the beginning of a long and dirty war in which the SAS would be forced to play a vital role in streets and fields that, to all intents and purposes, were identical to those they knew at home.

In the years that followed, SAS commanders accepted somewhat reluctantly, though without complaint, their deployment to the troubled province of Ulster, for the role they were called on to fulfil has always been restricted by political interference and the need to show results. It would be simplistic to suggest that the Regiment only works well in the shadows where the prying eyes of inquisitive journalists and the public cannot see, but SAS operations do rely heavily on secrecy, and this is drummed into the heads of every trooper from his first day in Hereford.

All soldiers serving in Northern Ireland, and that includes the SAS, are governed by the Yellow Card guidelines, which insist that a soldier may only open fire if his, or someone else's, life is in immediate danger. As any soldier or policeman who has seen real combat will tell you, it is frequently the person who shoots first who survives. The popular saying among soldiers who served in the province, 'better to be judged by twelve good men than to be carried by six' was, and is still a commonly held belief among soldiers serving there.

SAS officers normally serve a three-year tour with the Regiment and frequently move on to other postings, though some may return later after experience in different jobs. Consequently, several of the officers of other units posted to Northern Ireland had previously seen service with the SAS, and so brought with them SAS-style ideas.

When no arms shipments were discovered and the Regiment was withdrawn after the brief UVF alert, army covert operations remained. Military commanders on the ground had little faith in the value of RUC or Special Branch Intelligence and were eager to know as much as they could independently about what was happening on what they considered to be 'their ground'. With the army regiments that were posted to Northern Ireland came members of the Intelligence Corps, sometimes called the 'Int', though more commonly known to the SAS as the 'green slime', because of the colour of their berets.

The problem in those early days was that there was very little co-ordination between the army commanders stationed in the province, and the four-month tours of duty which most of the regiments served there left a vacuum during changeovers. In the early 1970s, numerous plain-clothed soldiers operated in Northern Ireland but to refer to them as covert operators would be wrong. Many ordinary officers and other ranks would go shopping in their free time in the centres of Belfast, Lisburn or Londonderry in civilian clothes wearing a shoulder holster and a 9mm Browning pistol, though few if any would ever fire one in action.

In 1969 there were fewer than 200 fully fledged members of the Official IRA, but encouraged by hardliners like the 19-year-old Gerry Adams, the Provos of the new Belfast PIRA Brigade began recruiting from the Catholic population Their terrorist war against the British was about to begin.

In Londonderry (or 'Derry', as most residents, especially Republicans, call it), a young Martin McGuinness disagreed with PIRA strategy and remained a firm supporter of the Stickies. This did not last for long, however. Soon he became an active member of PIRA, directed from Dublin by Sean MacStiofan and the seven-man Provisional Irish Republican Army Council.

PIRA's aim at the start of their campaign was to kill the same number of British soldiers in Northern Ireland as had died in Aden during the revolt there in the 1960s. Its Army Council believed this could cause a reaction among the population on the mainland leading to political embarrassment for the government and, if they were lucky, a withdrawal of British troops. Nothing, of course, could have been further from the truth, for if the British could accept the deaths of forty-four soldiers in Aden, it was most improbable that a similar loss in Northern Ireland would send them scurrying back to England. D Squadron by now were on their way to Oman and no members of the SAS would see Northern Ireland again until the mid-1970s.

In 1970, Brigadier (later General Sir) Frank Kitson, the newly appointed commander of 39 Brigade in Belfast who had served in counter-insurgency operations in Malaya, Kenya, Cyprus and Oman, approved the establishment of the Mobile Reconnaissance Force (MRF). Several of the recruits to this new force were of Irish origin, and were thus able to move relatively freely in the province without arousing suspicion. Even so, their work was extremely risky and the tasks they were given frequently involved operating under cover in highly sensitive areas where Republican or Loyalist gangs noticed strangers easily. Operating in sometimes rather scruffy unmarked cars, they would prowl the streets looking for suspected terrorists or watch potential bombing sites.

The unit was made up of around forty men and women soldiers who worked indirectly for the Secret Intelligence Service (MI6). Their activities included the use of massage parlours for gaining information, and the 'Four Square Laundry' van which cruised Republican areas. During one of these intelligence-gathering operations, a male and female soldier were fired on by a PIRA unit on the Twinbrook Estate, and the male soldier was killed. Agents run by the MRF were known as 'Freds', and during the early 1970s several of them who earned a reasonable living through informing, were assassinated by PIRA. A number of innocent men, accused by PIRA of being traitors to the cause also died during these early years of the Troubles.

When Sergeant Clive Williams, serving with the MRF, opened fire in Belfast's bus station on two men whom he claimed were armed, he ended up in court and the press had a field day. Adverse publicity in the Irish media revealed too many 'dirty tricks' for the liking of the British government of the day, and in early 1973 Kitson's ' secret army' was disbanded.

To fulfil the requirement for a covert special operations force in the province it was clear to British Intelligence (at that time Northern Ireland was MI6's responsibility) that a new and better co-ordinated force was needed. Between 1972 and 1974 a number of officers who had previously served tours with the SAS, as well as others from the Intelligence Corps, were posted to Northern Ireland where they operated in a role that seems to belong more in a novel by John le Carré than in a history of the British Army:

> Some of the things people got up to in the early seventies were real cloak-and-dagger affairs. Intelligence Corps officers and those seconded for covert ops worked very much on their own with very little accountability to the army's hierachy. An officer who was posted to Northern Ireland on special duties was very much his own man, and the MoD would sometimes rather not know the details. There were certainly conflicts of interest between the army and the other agencies operating in the province at that time, and that led to some serious arguments about who was giving the orders. It was a bit like James Bond without the palm trees or the dusky maidens.
>
> One of these covert ops guys, a major, used to frequent the Europa Hotel where the press stayed and drink with them into the early hours. Everyone liked him because he had a very quick wit and was never slow to buy a round. He even had a cottage in the country up in Antrim. This particular night everyone was

discussing the UVF and saying what a lot of wankers they were when suddenly a man dressed in a black suit and tie stands up and shouts 'Youse knows fuck all about the UVF!' and he throws something at the table. It's a button badge from the original UVF dating back to the First World War. Someone bought him a drink and he then told the reporters and the covert guy all about the current UVF set-up, what arms they had and so on. The result of what he said in his drunken state gave the Intelligence boys some useful info. It was often like that with people moving around the province unhindered by the strict rules that apply today.

The vacuum that was left in Ulster by the disbandment of the MRF was filled in 1974 with the creation of a new and highly secretive force, trained by the SAS and dedicated specifically to covert operations in Northern Ireland. This was 14 Intelligence Company, generally known as the Detachment or DET, and an account of the unit and its activities can be found at the end of this chapter.

For the RUC officers who policed the border areas the dawn of each day brought with it the risk of being gunned down either on or off duty:

At that time [the mid-1970s] we were still patrolling in ordinary cars with no real protection. A few of us had bullet-proof jackets borrowed from the army, but in fact these were just flak vests like the ones the Yanks had in Vietnam. They wouldn't stop a bullet. There was one guy driving a police Cortina down a lane in South Armagh with the observer in the passenger seat and another chap in the back with the Stirling sub-machine gun. They didn't know what hit them. The car was ambushed as they came down the road and high-velocity fire ripped through the doors and windows. The next moment the driver's sitting there with his observer's head in his lap, blood and brains everywhere. He was only a young fellow, the driver. That's him over there in the corner staring into his pint.

An advance party of twelve men from D Squadron who had just completed a tour in Oman established their headquarters at the army helicopter base at Bessbrook Mill in South Armagh.

By announcing the presence of the SAS in Ulster, Harold Wilson was playing a dangerous game of one-upmanship specifically designed to frighten the terrorists out of South Armagh. It made things especially dangerous for the SAS, who prefer their governments not to announce their travel arrangements to the world's press, which is exactly what Wilson did. Some of the men who took part in those early operations expressed their displeasure at having been used in this way, and a number of deception plans had to be implemented to confuse the enemy.

The propaganda war had already begun in Northern Ireland some years earlier, but now the Special Air Service was thrown into a role for which it was never originally intended. From the start of their deployment in South Armagh, it was unclear who exactly had charge of what the SAS men were supposed to be doing. Contrary to some reports, they did not go out on regular patrols with other army units, or assassinate dozens of PIRA volunteers and bury them in unmarked graves. During their deployment to the border areas in 1976 and 1977 the SAS squadron killed two members of a PIRA active service unit (ASU), Seamus Harvey and Peter Joseph Cleary, and captured many others including a PIRA commander, Sean McKenna, who was believed to have been responsible for planning many of the sectarian killings at that time.

The Regiment's 'wanted list' identified ten key PIRA operatives who, according to British Intelligence were responsible for directing most of the sectarian killings and attacks on security forces in the border areas. By the end of 1976 the Regiment had accounted for four of the PIRA group and the others had fled south.

PIRA terrorists frequently committed their raids in the north and ran back over the border to the relative safety of the Irish Republic, and this the SAS knew was where they would be at their most vulnerable. In any other conflict, the Regiment would have simply studied the map and worked out the logistics involved for crossing the border, but in this particularly sensitive conflict there would be serious political repercussions if their presence was noticed in Eire.

Just before 11 pm on the night of 5 May 1976, a policeman from the Irish Garda Síochána stopped a civilian car at Cornamucklagh in the Republic of Ireland. Inside the vehicle he found four men with British accents, including a Fijian. In the car he also discovered a variety of weapons, and he therefore immediately called for reinforcements. The men explained that they were British soldiers, but this did not impress the garda. He had bagged an interesting catch and there could well be promotion for him when his superiors heard about this.

Within minutes two other unmarked cars arrived at the scene containing more 'Englishmen', but despite the explanation that the first group had made 'a map-reading error' and that they were all brothers in the fight against terrorism, the gardaí were adamant that they were under arrest. The temptation to fight their way out of this embarrassing predicament must have been tremendous but the SAS men were forced to recognize the sensitivity of the situation and resigned themselves to a night in the cells.

In all, the Garda Síochána had nabbed eight members of the SAS, three cars, four Stirling sub-machine guns, a pump-action shotgun and three Browning pistols. The fact that nine Republican terrorists had tunnelled out of the Maze prison that same day and that a car stolen in Forkhill, South Armagh, had spirited away six of them that night, had nothing to do with the incident, claimed the British Army's press office in Lisburn.

After some hectic behind-the-scenes night-time activity by Whitehall – and a lot of red faces – the men were released and flown back to England. The SAS had learnt a bitter lesson, for they knew that the only way to defeat terrorism was to operate deep inside the enemy's territory, and the political will that would enable them to do that was not there. If they crossed the border they would be on their own and without the approval of their government. Some concluded that they were being expected to fight a war with their hands tied behind their backs, and that all the advantages lay with the terrorists.

Sir Kenneth Newman, the newly appointed Chief Constable of the RUC, admired the obvious skills of the SAS and saw a use for them in the province, but he was insistent that the rule of law must always apply in a democracy. He ordered that the SAS must abide by the rules, and took the view that its soldiers should be kept in reserve for covert intelligence-gathering operations in rural areas and for confronting PIRA units who were planning or implementing major operations.

In the final analysis Newman was responsible for law and order in Northern Ireland, and it was difficult for him to justify the illegal activities of British soldiers. Whichever way one looks at it, crossing national frontiers and kidnapping people is against the law. If the Regiment were forbidden by law from taking the war to the terrorists, they would just have to put themselves in the line of fire and trust in their training and experience to get the better of the gunmen. Operating like this, though, could easily go wrong, as one SAS man nearly found out to his cost:

> Myself in civvies, and an SB [Special Branch] man were having a drink in a pub on the border in Armagh waiting for the IRA to call. We'd had a tip-off that they were going to shoot up the place, though usually these things didn't work out the way they were expected to. I was sitting at a low table with my back to the wall, facing the door. After a long wait and a few drinks it happened. Suddenly he comes bursting in wearing a big heavy coat and he's raising the old Thompson sub-machine gun [the 'Tommy' gun once the standard weapon of the 1930s American gangsters]. I started moving, going for this little Walther 7.65mm in an ankle holster. As I'm coming into the aim position, although I didn't aim, there wasn't time for that, we heard this loud 'clunk'. Can you imagine that? His Thompson had misfired. There he was, trying to clear his gun, have another go at everyone, spray the place and I was putting rounds into him. I fired the full magazine, hit him I'm sure seven times as he was realizing he'd better give up. He was turning and heading out through the door. I reloaded and looked at this little Walther with its hopeless stopping power as the gunman dived into a car and took off across the border. It was the coat that was absorbing the bullets . . . he just wouldn't fall down.

The gunman had indeed been hit seven times, and died later in Eire.

Despite the restrictions placed on them, D Squadron succeeded in bringing a qualified peace to the troubled border areas, if only for a while. Prime Minister Harold Wilson's plan had worked, and for a long time following the deployment of D Squadron, PIRA assassins suspected the SAS of hiding behind every bush.

The men and women of the Royal Ulster Constabulary who face sudden death at the hands of gunmen and bombers each day, and who are most vulnerable when they are off duty, also formed their own counter-terrorist teams. The Special Patrol Group's Bronze Section, set up in 1976, operated in unmarked cars in high-risk areas and reported directly to the RUC's Special Branch headquarters at Knock. Sporting, in some cases, long hair and beards and looking more like navvies than policemen, Bronze Section teams had several notable successes in the terrorist war, especially in Loyalist areas where they managed to blend in easily with the city's hard men. However, after some notorious mishaps caused mainly by the lack of organization, the RUC decided it needed a properly trained and equipped unit of its own, comparable to the army's DET.

The Operations Division of RUC Special Branch, E4,[3] gave birth to E4A, a specially trained surveillance unit designed to operate covertly gathering intelligence in the province, and using the latest technological wizardry supplied by the Security Service, MI5. Meanwhile E4 members were sent on firearms training courses to SAS Headquarters in Hereford, where they learnt advanced shooting and tactical skills. 14 Intelligence Company personnel also attended these courses, though some of the SAS instructors were unconvinced that the RUC and 14 Int. students possessed the qualities needed for 'keeni-meeni' operations.[4]

[3] RUC Special Branch (E Department) has other units: E1 is responsible for transport, administration, etc.; E2 is the Legal Division; E3 is the Intelligence unit.

[4] Keeni-meeni' – from the Swahili, meaning the movement of a snake in the grass, and hence covert operations as practised by the SAS in Aden.

In the mid 1970s Sir Kenneth Newman created the Tasking and Co-ordination Group (TCG) which brought together police, Special Branch and army security experts. The role of the TCG was to examine the latest collated intelligence, and decide what action should be taken to respond to terrorist activities, or more importantly, try to be one jump ahead of them.

One of the first attempts to hit the terrorists before they themselves could strike ended in disaster in July 1978. An SAS team stationed at an army base in County Antrim had been assigned to watch a terrorist arms cache in a graveyard in Dunloy. The SAS men were told by RUC Special Branch that it was believed that the cache was part of a PIRA operation to attack a Loyalist march two days later. Despite warnings by the police to the local farmer, who had tipped them off in the first place, his son, John Boyle, turned up at the graveyard, took a rifle from its hiding place and was promptly shot dead by the SAS team.

Two other RUC units came into being in 1980, the Divisional Mobile Support Unit (DMSU) and the Headquarters Mobile Support Unit (HMSU), both of which were intended for rapid response to threats, and were similar to England's (or Northern Ireland's) old Special Patrol Group (SPG). Both these groups received British army firearms training in England, mostly in Aldershot. A third force, the Special Support Unit (SSU), was created in the same year. Many of the SSU officers came from the old Bronze Section of the disbanded SPG, and these men received firearms training from the SAS in Hereford.

In brief, the SAS was happy to offer training to the RUC because it meant that their own workload in Northern Ireland could be substantially reduced, and that they would be held in reserve for the serious job of

123

tackling the terrorists on their own terms. Lying in a hidden OP on the border for weeks, in the rain, was perfectly normal work for an SAS trooper, but with the advances in surveillance technology and the collation of intelligence through informers, this was becoming less necessary. But the combat skills of the RUC's special units did not match those of the SAS, and in 1982 a series of bungled incidents led to the Stalker 'shoot-to-kill' inquiry.

In the course of two months and in three separate incidents, six Catholics were gunned down in Armagh by special RUC units, and the circumstances of the deaths led to some serious questions being asked in Westminster. The fact that two of the victims belonged to PIRA and two were members of the Irish National Liberation Army (INLA, a breakaway Republican paramilitary organization)) did little to calm the waters, for it seemed from the evidence that each man had been killed without being given a chance to surrender, and no weapons were found on them. The repercussions of the Stalker investigations led Whitehall and the security forces to re-examine the whole counter-terrorist strategy in Northern Ireland. The men in charge realized that if they were to win the media war and the 'hearts and minds' of the public there could be no more mistakes.

The reality was that in spite of high-grade intelligence, be it SIGINT (signals intelligence) or HUMINT (human intelligence), and high levels of special operations training and discipline, mistakes could always happen. The nature of the work carried out by SAS soldiers in Northern Ireland might involve days or months of waiting for something to happen, and when it did, the actions often lasted only a few adrenalin-packed seconds. From 1976, when D Squadron was first deployed in the province, until 1988, the SAS shot dead thirty-one people. Six of these were accidental killings or shootings of individuals caught in crossfire, an average of less than three killings per year, or one every four months. In fact there were long periods of inaction when a trooper on station in Northern Ireland might see no combat at all. Between February 1985 and April 1987, the Regiment was responsible for the killing of only one PIRA member, when, in April 1986, Seamus McElwaine was shot dead in County Fermanagh.

Having learnt by some of their mistakes, E Department (RUC Special Branch) and MI5 on the mainland directed their collated intelligence through the TCG and tasked the SAS with specific actions that suited their precise skills. E Department's own personnel were more than competent at gathering and sifting the daily mass of intelligence flowing from HUMINT or SIGINT sources, and dealing with the bands of informers who were looking for a way out of the endless nightmare of terrorism.

With DET (14 Int.) constantly on hand and able to hit the enemy very hard, and with a high degree of skill, the security forces by the early 1980s felt sufficiently capable of controlling almost any terrorist threat. In situations which appeared to be beyond the capabilities of DET or the RUC's own SSUs, the SAS could be rapidly deployed to squadron strength in less than two hours. As a further guarantee, the Regiment maintained a unit of troop strength on six-month tours in the province, which operated in liaison with an E Department chief inspector and personnel from other agencies. Known simply as 'the Troop', its members were drawn from the Regiment's squadrons in rotation and to bring them up to date with developments and changes in Northern Ireland, each man would team up for a brief period with a local DET soldier on his arrival. In 1985, however, following an embarrassing incident in County Tyrone when three members of G Squadron took a wrong turning and had to escape from a hostile Republican mob on foot, abandoning their unmarked car and its contents, which included a weapon, the SAS operations in Northern Ireland were subjected to a major reassessment. As a result of this the troop-sized contingent was replaced by a new, slightly larger, all-volunteer team, whose members would serve a twelve-month posting. Competition among volunteers was fierce and when the final choices were made, some of the Regiment's most experienced and courageous soldiers received the postings. Since their first deployment in force in 1976, the Regiment has had a number of impressive successes against the Provisional IRA and the INLA, as well as several less-publicized ones, and has suffered very few casualties. Only two members of the Regiment have died in action in the province. Captain Richard Westmacott was shot dead while approaching a PIRA ambush in north Belfast in 1980, and Lance Corporal Alastair Slater was killed in a firefight near Kesh, County Fermanagh, in 1984. Another SAS man, Tommy Palmer, who won the Queen's Gallantry Medal at the Iranian Embassy siege, was killed in a car crash on a motorway near Lurgan in 1983.

The Regiment's biggest and most publicized coup against PIRA came in the spring of 1987. On 25 April the Provisionals blew up the car of Lord Justice Maurice Gibson as it crossed the border in South Armagh. The 500-pound bomb, hidden at the side of the road, killed the judge and his wife, Cecily, outright. The couple were on their way home from holiday but due to several recent attacks on RUC patrols in the area, it had been decided to discontinue their usual police escort.

Fourteen days later, on 8 May, a PIRA active service unit launched a daring attack on the police station in Loughgall, eight miles north of Armagh city. Led by Jim

Lynagh, a battle-scarred veteran of many previous PIRA campaigns, the eight-man unit planned to ram the gates of the RUC base with a JCB digger containing a 500-pound bomb.

Lynagh had been released from Portlaoise prison, Eire, in 1986. He had been a Sinn Fein councillor, and had served five years in Long Kesh. In 1982 he had been sentenced to five years' imprisonment in the Republic for possession of illegal ammunition. What Lynagh and his volunteers did not know was that the security forces had built up a detailed picture of the Fermanagh, Tyrone and Armagh PIRA units. RUC Special Branch knew most of the names of the members of these units, had photographs of them, and were constantly updating their intelligence.

Better liaison between RUC Special Branch and their counterparts in the Garda Síochána now meant that, when PIRA gunmen went south into Eire, they were not safe. Following a series of attacks on police stations in the border areas in 1986 and early 1987, information received and analysed by the TCG indicated that an attack was imminent and that Loughgall was the target.

Knowing Jim Lynagh's preference for working with large groups and PIRA's growing fear of the security forces' covert-operations teams, it seemed probable that the attack would involve a relatively large number of terrorists. The resident SAS troop in Northern Ireland was therefore quickly reinforced with men from G Squadron who were at that time on Special Projects/CRW duties. Flown in from Hereford, their orders were to set up an 'OP/React',[5] and the operation was to be codenamed 'Judy'.

Intelligence sources had located a large cache of explosives in a farm a few kilometres away from

[5] 'OP/React' – observation post able to react; an ambush.

Loughgall, and when a blue Toyota Hiace van was hijacked in Dungannon, and shortly afterwards a digger was stolen from a farm, the TCG went on full alert. In the early evening of Friday, 8 May the digger was seen when it turned up at the farm where the explosives were cached. The SAS, numbering almost forty men, were already on the ground in different locations, some of them positioned inside the police station at Loughgall.

Using the finely honed surveillance techniques that the resident troop had developed with MI5 over the years of conflict in Northern Ireland, and with Special Branch's HUMINT playing a key role, the security forces were able to ensure that Lynagh's PIRA attack was doomed before it started. Equipped with secure radio communications and formidable firepower, the SAS men lay in wait. Just before 7:15 pm the Toyota van drove down the hill towards the police station. It passed, made a U-turn and went back up the hill. Moments later it returned, this time followed by the digger. On reaching the police station, three PIRA men got out of the van and opened fire with automatic weapons. Another went to light the fuse of the 500-pound bomb with his Zippo lighter, and at almost the same moment the first SAS man fired.

In the seconds that followed and as the bomb exploded, the PIRA unit in the 'killing zone' was raked with a withering torrent of high-velocity rounds from the SAS's Heckler and Koch G3-A4Ks and GPMGs. In the heat of the action which is too often the reality of combat, two innocent local men were caught in crossfire. Wearing overalls similar to those of the PIRA unit, Anthony Hughes died and his brother Oliver was seriously wounded as they tried to reverse their car away from the shooting. Mistaking them for terrorists

Members of D Squadron aboard their Willys jeep near Poitiers, France, during Operation Bulbasket, June 1944. Armed with four powerful Vickers 'K' machine guns, these behind-the-lines SAS teams had a devastating effect on enemy morale.
© Anthony Kemp

Above: David Stirling, or 'D.S.' to his friends, wearing his favourite duffel coat in the North African Desert. The patrol of Willys jeeps behind him is equipped with twin Vickers 'K' machine guns, spare petrol and water. As 'Andy McNab' and his patrol Bravo Two-Zero discovered, the desert at night can be bitterly cold.

© T. Nevill/The Defence Picture Library

Right: An SAS soldier wearing his sand-coloured beret and 'Sword of Damocles' badge. In 1996 the SAS Regimental Association announced that this was the original and correct title for the badge, not 'The Winged Dagger'. He is armed with one of the SAS's favourite weapons, the American M16A1 5.56mm assault rifle. He is wearing an SAS windproof smock and a 'headover' round his neck.

© Peter Russell/The Military Picture Library

Above: The Regiment's jungle training course in Brunei is one of the most strenuous exercises in the British Army. Here two members of a patrol are 'buttoned up' against thorns and 'creepy-crawlies'. They are carrying the '203', an M16A1 rifle and M203 launcher which fires a variety of 40mm grenades, including high-explosive, air-burst and white phosphorous.

© Stephen McConnell/The Military Picture Library

Left: Gliding in towards his target, an SAS 'HALO' trooper prepares to land using his steerable parachute. The Regiment has practised insertion of its troops behind enemy lines from many types of aircraft, including civilian airliners, from heights of more than 25,000 feet.

© Jim Perkins/The Defence Picture Library

Right: Clutching an American M1 carbine and his trusty meerschaum pipe, popular with many SAS soldiers, a sergeant has his kit checked during the Malayan Emergency. 'Tree jumping' where soldiers parachuted into the thick jungle canopy and abseiled to the ground was finally abandoned. Even for the SAS, it was considered too dangerous.

© Crown copyright PTS Museum/The Military Picture Library

Below: 'It's simply a question of mind over matter. Keep your mind working, your feet moving, and the rest doesn't matter.' A soldier carries an L1A1 Self-Loading Rifle (SLR) during SAS Selection with the summits of Pen-Y-Fan and Corn Du in the distance. Day-Glo orange signal panels are attached to the top of bergens so Directing Staff (DS) can spot soldiers when visibility is poor.

© Kirk Bain/The Military Picture Library

Left: A member of the Australian SAS Regiment near a drop zone at dusk; armed like many of his British counterparts with an M16, he is wearing Australian 'designed-by-computer' camouflage 'that really works!' Many Australian SAS soldiers fought in South Vietnam during the late 1960s and early 1970s.

© Antony Rogers/The Military Picture Library

Below: In the long grass - often a better place to site an OP than a wood or buildings. Many SAS soldiers cut off part of the brim of their jungle hats to give better all-round vision. This soldier (who hasn't) waits in an ambush position with a '203', an M16A1 fitted with an M203 grenade launcher.

© Stephen McConnell/The Military Picture Library

Above: With his M16 Colt Commando within arm's reach, an SAS signaller types out a message on a Merod data encryption keyboard. When coded, he sends it in high-speed morse on a PRC319 radio.

© Peter Russell/The Military Picture Library

Left: 'If you get a kink in it, it may break.' A survival expert demonstrating the right and wrong way of using a wire saw to cut wood. If the end loops are removed, the saw can be slipped inside the draw-string of a coat or hood, a trick taught to recruits on escape and evasion exercises.
© Tim Fisher/The Military Picture Library

Below: Members of the Special Boat Service (SBS) 'fast-roping' on to the roof of the British Embassy in Kuwait following the Iraqi army's withdrawal. Similar to, but more exciting than abseiling, fast-roping employs a much thicker rope, and the soldier slides down it like a fireman using a fireman's pole. 'You're so scared, you never let go,' says one connoisseur.
© MU/Reynolds/The Defence Picture Library

Above: At the rear of the Iranian Embassy in London members of B Squadron prepare to abseil from the roof at the start of Operation Nimrod. During the long siege, SAS men jogged around Hyde Park to keep fit. © T. Nevill/The Defence Picture Library

Below: Members of 21 Regiment SAS based at the Duke of York's Barracks, Chelsea, London, waiting to board a Hercules C130 for a practice night drop. Their main parachutes are the Irvin PX Mk4, and the reserves PR7s. The second man from the right and several others are wearing their issue SAS windproof smocks (see Chapter Four – Weapons and Equipment).
© Peter Russell/The Military Picture Library

trying to escape, the SAS riddled their car with fire. Another car being driven up the hill by a woman stopped as the bullets flew past her. Seeing the danger, an SAS man dashed to the car and led the woman and her daughter to safety. He was later awarded the Military Medal for his bravery.

PIRA members Paddy Kelly, Declan Arthurs, Seamus Donnelly, Gerard O'Callaghan, Tony Gormley, Patrick McKearney, Eugene Kelly and Jim Lynagh lay dead. Armoured vests worn by Lynagh and McKearney had not saved them. Less than thirty minutes after the action, the SAS team had left the area by helicopter.

More than a year later, on 1 July 1988, a PIRA attack on North Queen Street RUC barracks ended again in disaster. Firing an RPG-7 (rocket-propelled grenade, launched from a tube) at the building, the three-man unit drove into another SAS trap. When their car was later found abandoned, police discovered blood-stained clothing inside, but the PIRA men had fled.

The Detachment

The 14th Intelligence and Security Company is usually known as 'the Detachment', though soldiers serving in Northern Ireland and the SAS refer to it simply as the DET. The idea for the creation of this new and very secret organization came from an SAS major who had retired from the army and joined the Secret Intelligence Service (MI6). His task, which began in 1972, was to select and train members of the British armed forces for covert operations in an environment where the local population was constantly aware of strangers, most especially Englishmen. One veteran of those early operations recalls:

Each city area, be it Protestant or Catholic, is like a walled encampment though frequently you couldn't see the wall. Over the years a tribal map marked in orange (Protestants), green (Catholics), and grey (mixed areas) was issued to troops serving in cities like Belfast and Londonderry giving the blokes an idea of where one enclave ended and another began. Nothing moved in places like the Shankill, the Ardoyne, Andersonstown, the Bogside or the Creggan without the locals knowing so it was a waste of time sending in a car full of squaddies from Birmingham to have a look for the cut-throats and bombers. Trying to mimic their accents was also a waste of time and usually ended in disaster with blokes running for their car with a mob of mad 'millies' [loud-mouthed women] after them. What was needed was a new approach. DET had some good ideas but most especially excellent leadership.

The selection course, although extremely thorough, was not as physically demanding as the SAS version, for a different sort of soldier was required. DET personnel were tested for their powers of observation and memory, their ability to analyse data and assess potentially dangerous situations, and their capacity for blending into their surroundings.

The SAS did, however, undertake the job of training DET members in Hereford in some of the Regiment's specialized skills, training which included a modified SAS selection course with treks across the Welsh hills, close-quarter battle tactics, and resistance to interrogation training. DET members, both men and women, had to excel in the ancient hunter's arts of camouflage and concealment and be as good at that as any SAS man. Operating from concealed OPs in a city requires a special kind of ingenuity that is rarely found in the average soldier, but these were only some of the talents DET personnel needed in order to stay alive.

A great amount of effort was put into teaching recruits advanced surveillance techniques and the intelligent and rather less rigid military-style use of modern telecommunications. This would enable them to keep in touch with their bases and each other, use the minimum amount of 'air-time' possible and thus reduce the risk of eavesdroppers interpreting their actions, or identifying their areas of operation. Even though there were several so-called 'secure' radio sets in use in the province at that time, as there are today, this would not stop PIRA from monitoring SAS and DET communications.

On one occasion, following a raid on a house in Belfast, a complex radio eavesdropping system was found in the attic. A PIRA unit, including a university graduate with an impressive knowledge of telecommunications, had been listening to the SAS's radio traffic. To combat this threat, a complex radio code was created enabling operators to identify suspects or locations to each other without mentioning them by name. Keeping individuals or buildings under observation without DET hideouts or vehicles being noticed was an art that had to be learnt in urban, suburban or rural environments, each of which needed very specific skills.

Using concealed, state-of-the-art video cameras fitted with fibre-optic lenses, DET operatives would carefully position cars or vans to watch suspects' homes, vehicles or areas of their activity, then return, sometimes days later, to drive the vehicle away and analyse the video tapes. Wherever possible, a watcher would be supported by a back-up quick-reaction force (QRF), and rather than using fully armoured and bullet-proof vehicles which might be spotted by a suspicious local, certain parts of these cars or vans, such as the seats and headrests and doors, were reinforced with Kevlar. These dangerous covert missions required nerves of steel from the DET teams during the insertion and exfiltration phases, and an ability to appear at home in their surroundings was vital.

Captain Tony Ball was the unit's first commander. Ball had worked his way up through the ranks of the Parachute Regiment before passing SAS selection, but had left to take up a commission in the King's Own Scottish Borderers. It was during a tour with the KOSBs in the early 1970s that he began to 'get a feel' for the complex and difficult anti-terrorist war in Ulster, and he showed a natural flair for the kind of work that DET had been designed for.

Ball's liaison officer was Lieutenant Robert Nairac, a young Guards officer with a reputation for being able to handle himself in tight situations. Like David Stirling, Nairac had been educated at the Catholic college of Ampleforth before going up to Oxford (Stirling was at Cambridge) where he became a boxing blue. Captain (later Lieutenant-Colonel) Julian Anthony Ball, KOSB, died in a road accident in Dhofar in 1978 and is buried in the SAS graveyard in Hereford. On 15 May 1977, Robert Nairac, then a captain, was kidnapped and murdered by PIRA following a fierce struggle in the car park of a Republican pub near the Irish border.

While the early work carried out by members of the unit was without doubt extremely skilful and courageous, the effect it had in the PSYOPS (psychological operations) war against the terrorist was devastating. His safe havens were no longer safe. Now there were eyes and ears watching him as he relaxed in the local pub or nipped down to the corner shop for a packet of cigarettes. His friends were identified and their movements carefully logged, and except for a few rare cases where DET teams were compromised, he could not see the watchers. Since their creation, DET personnel have been awarded more than a hundred medals for bravery in Northern Ireland – far more, in fact, than have been awarded to the SAS.

Since the British Army's first deployment in Ulster in 1969, those paramilitaries from both Republican and Loyalist camps who had a good knowledge of Britain's military machine had anticipated that the SAS would be used against them. It made sense that such a force would be called upon as they were the ideal troops for the job of combating terrorism. What PIRA did not know was that another special army force had been created with the sole purpose of taking on both them and their loyalist UVF enemies in a covert war. This explains why for many years communiqués from PIRA in Dublin and statements and obituaries in *An Phoblact*[6] blamed the SAS for having 'murdered their volunteers'. The Ministry of Defence rarely identifies a special forces group following the shooting of gunmen or bombers, and this leaves a valuable element of doubt and confusion in the minds of the media and of the terrorist.

In 1974 there was a dangerous development in the intelligence war in Ulster when a dispute between the Secret Intelligence Service (MI6) and the Security Service (MI5) came to a head. RUC Special Branch, which works directly to MI5 and runs a complex network of informers, resented the fact that British Army Intelligence had an ever-increasing number of operations and informers of its own and was dealing directly with MI6. At that time each major RUC station had a liaison officer from the army, a field intelligence NCO

[6] *An Phoblact* or *Republican News* is the official newspaper of Sinn Féin and PIRA.

(FINCO) whose job it was to inform the RUC of military operations in the area and pass on RUC information to the army. At the same time the RUC's SB officers were running agents in both the north and the south of Ireland and liaising informally with detectives from the Garda Síochána's Special Branch.

The result ended in disaster for several of MI6's Republican informers, and when ten of that agency's best sources were murdered by PIRA, the army liaison officer who had run several of them as agents committed suicide.

From 1974 onwards, despite a number of secret talks between MI6 and representatives of PIRA, MI5 became responsible for all of Britain's covert operations against Irish terrorist groups, while MI6 returned to its original role of directing overseas security and intelligence operations.

When documents relating to a 'Doomsday Plan' were discovered in a raid on one of PIRA's safe houses in Belfast, Harold Wilson's Labour government began to realize that it would take more than an intelligence-gathering network, the RUC and a handful of DET people to counter terrorism in Ulster. Wilson approved the setting up of army close-observation platoons (COPs) in each of the regiments posted there. Gradually SAS surveillance methods were being taught to a wide variety of ordinary soldiers, although not by the SAS. This did not mean, however, that those soldiers had the necessary character or skills to carry out covert operations, though many may have thought of themselves at the time as being 'special forces'.

Although the SAS made a brief appearance in 1974 when a small detachment from B Squadron[7] was deployed to the province, their most widely publicized operation began in January 1976 following a series of sectarian killings in the 'bandit country' of South Armagh. In the six months leading up to the SAS's deployment, twenty-four civilians and forty-nine members of the security forces had been murdered in a frenzy of uncontrollable violence by both Republican and Loyalist terrorists.

[7] The brief 1974 tour ended badly when two SAS men robbed a bank in Londonderry. Both were jailed for six years.

SEVEN

SHE WHO DARES WINS

At a secret location somewhere in Northern Ireland, the members of a counter-terrorist unit are preparing for an undercover operation which, if all goes according to plan, will place them face to face with an armed active service unit of the Provisional IRA. One of them, a female volunteer, has the most dangerous job. Her task is to position a surveillance car fitted with a concealed video camera outside a suspect's home address. If she can find a convenient place to park she will set the camera running, whisper into a radio microphone concealed in her collar that the car is in position, then quietly slip away trying not to be noticed. Whatever happens she has to remain calm and in total control of her actions. The least hesitation – fumbling with the car keys, for example – might be noticed. Around the corner at a prearranged rendezvous point chosen from detailed aerial photographs and out of sight of the target house, another team member will pick her up and drive her away. Their timing must be impeccable. The pair will repeat the operation in reverse before sunset, for when night falls, strangers' cars have a habit of being stripped and set alight or borrowed by joyriders.

But why has a woman been chosen for such a hazardous mission? The answer is simple and would soon be obvious to any male outsider who cared to go for a stroll or drive around any of Northern Ireland's hard-line Republican or Loyalist areas. Within minutes of his arrival a man would be noticed and challenged. The story will be the same on Lenadoon Avenue in Repub-lican Andersonstown or Downing Street on the Loyal-ist Shankill Road. It may be inquisitive children asking probing questions – 'Hey mister, who are you?' – or it might be their mothers with their hair in curlers chasing the intruder down the street and yelling, 'See your man there? He's a peeler!'[1] Such women can be the most blatantly aggressive of antagonists, and the worst threat of compromising SAS-style 'keeni-meeni' operations (see p. 122). If the stranger has no good reason for being there, and if this is not his lucky day, the challenger may be a young man, usually aged less than thirty, with a pis-tol tucked into the waistband of his trousers, hidden under his jacket. Unless the uninvited visitor can legiti-mately explain his presence he may be taken for a spy and find himself running for his life. At worst he would end up with a plastic shopping bag on his head and a bullet drilled through his skull. If he has an English accent his chances of convincing the locals that he is not a member of the security forces are very slim.

Twenty years ago, before high technology surveil-lance equipment was as advanced as it is today, a covert operations soldier would sometimes hide in the boot of a car for hours in order to watch the homes of suspected terrorists through a tiny hole in the bodywork; that, however, would only have occurred if there were no convenient derelict buildings to hide in. The enemy had got used to battered vans and unknown cars appearing near their front doors at odd hours. Sometimes such

[1] Nineteenth-century English slang for a policeman; still used in Ulster.

137

vehicles would be attacked by children and their mothers with stones, slates and bottles, and more dangerously by young PIRA volunteers armed with Molotov cocktails or automatic weapons. Many times undercover operators had to be rescued by uniformed army units, backing their armoured Pig up to the front or back door of an abandoned house with mobs of angry residents bombarding the soldiers with bricks.

To function successfully in the 'spying-on-terrorists' business today requires lots of cunning and some very original ideas. Several operators have died, believing themselves well hidden behind camouflage and scrim nets in makeshift hides in the corners of Northern Irish fields, or when they were spotted cruising around high-risk city areas in unmarked cars. But the enemy haven't always had things their own way. Several of this woman operator's comrades have won medals for gallantry in fierce shoot-outs with terrorists.

In Londonderry one spring afternoon, an undercover colleague driving alone in an unmarked brown Opel Ascona car was chased by four PIRA men in a hijacked Ford Escort. The gunmen's car overtook the Opel, forcing it to a halt. The soldier managed to keep his cool, letting one of the Armalite-carrying terrorists walk up to his driver's window while another covered him and walked to the rear of his car. The soldier got out of the car and stood behind his door. When the gunman demanded to know the plain-clothed soldier's identity, he calmly reached behind the sun visor and pulled out his driving licence. As the first gunman turned away to inspect it, the soldier seized his chance. Fast-drawing his Browning pistol, he pumped nine quick rounds into twenty-four-year-old George McBrearty, who returned fire as he fell, splashing blood across the open door of the Opel. The soldier then swung round to his right and double-tapped two rounds into the face of Charles 'Pop' Maguire, aged twenty. Both McBrearty and Maguire died where they fell.

Racing away with his car tyres screeching, the soldier then opened fire on the Ford Escort, hitting one of the other gunmen. They caught the wounded man later with five 9mm bullets in him, and he received a paltry five-year jail sentence for possession of an illegal weapon. Just one little Browning against all those Armalites: if the soldier's gun had jammed, or if he had hesitated for a split second it would have been another story. Using skill-at-arms and cool judgement he had survived against impossible odds.

Today's covert operation would be just as risky, but the closely knit undercover team has methodically developed and refined their techniques in an effort to reduce the risks. The back-up units would be close, though not close enough to draw attention to themselves, or for that matter close enough to do much if the girl parking the car were challenged. Then, just like the soldier who had narrowly escaped with his life, she would be on her own, at least for a few, adrenalin-packed seconds.

Wearing jeans, a sweater and an old battered jacket, Kate (not her real name) is in her early twenties, and speaks with a Northern English accent. She has spent a long time with a girlfriend, another member of her team, carefully choosing what to wear. Clothing has to be functional and plain enough not to attract attention. She checks her silhouette in the mirror, making sure there is no tell-tale bulge from the 9mm Browning Hi-Power pistol hidden under her left arm in its quick-release holster, and the state-of-the-art 'secure comms' transceiver, her only life-line to the outside world should anything go wrong.

Clothing is a major problem. The medical officer has advised them to wear natural fibres like cotton and wool which are much better materials for digging out of blast injuries or gunshot wounds. Nylon and other man-made fabrics have a nasty tendency to melt, bubbling and burning into the skin, a positive nightmare for a surgeon trying to save a casualty's life. Like the men, she has experimented with various holsters, slings, pockets and pouches for carrying her equipment. Some of the kit-carrying systems – tailor-made waistcoats with pouches for everything including her pistol, spare magazines, radio, saline-drip and giving set, water bottle and first field dressings – were extremely good, but they required the wearing of an enormous coat in order to hide everything. If the sun came out and you started to sweat, things got very uncomfortable. Baling out of a car and joining pedestrians in shirtsleeves when you are wearing an enormous Barbour jacket or a duffle coat looks extremely suspicious, is very hot, and is guaranteed to make people look at you.

Some of the old hands had developed their own ingenious techniques with concealed holsters for carrying the Heckler & Koch MP5-K under a coat, but the more easily concealed 'semi' was still the most valuable item for personal protection. Some of them preferred the feel of the pistol close to their body, tucked into their waistband just like some of their PIRA enemies. Whatever clothing and kit-carrying equipment this female volunteer chooses to wear, she has to be able to run easily in it. Shoes, boots or trainers need to be of a close fit so they will not slip off, be tightly laced and have a good grip.

One last glance in the mirror to check her appearance. Who knows? If luck is against her this could be her last dangerous mission. Maybe she won't beat the clock this time. She has been into the same area on several occasions during this tour of duty, and it is surely only a matter of time before one of them notices her.

Holding the Browning pistol flat in the upturned palm of her right hand, she slips a full and very carefully loaded magazine into the handgrip, hears the reassuring click, then pulls the slide back smoothly, releasing it abruptly. There is a metallic crash as the slide slams forward, chambering the uppermost 9mm parabellum round in the breech. She flicks on the safety catch. Soldiers in Northern Ireland are not supposed to cock their weapons – which is what she has just done – until their lives are in imminent danger, but all the members of her team know that such well-meaning rules could cost you your life in the split-second action of a sudden contact. She checks her cheap but reliable wristwatch, not the G10 stores-issued one which would identify her instantly as a soldier, and inhales deeply on a last cigarette. How many 'coffin nails' today, she wonders? She really should give them up as they're bad for her health.

Opening the door of the bleak Nissen hut she carries out a quick radio check with the male team member heading towards her and then walks confidently, almost too confidently, in the teeming rain towards the Q-car. In less than an hour she will be driving into the city with the others in a staggered convoy, keeping radio communications to an absolute minimum, and preparing herself for phase one of an operation that may last just one day or could run for several weeks. Either way, it's better than working, like her sister, in a factory making ladies' underwear, even if it might result in sudden, violent death.

If anyone had suggested to Stirling's 'Originals' in 1941 that a bunch of good-looking, pistol-packing girls might one day be taking part in SAS operations and aiming sub-machine guns at their country's enemies, he would have been dismissed with a typically chauvinistic chuckle of disbelief. More probably, the person would have received a swift punch to the nose for insulting David Stirling's and Paddy Mayne's intrepid warriors. But that was precisely what happened, and until recently it was one of the SAS's best kept secrets. Those who work in the offices of the Ministry of Defence in Whitehall, though sometimes accused of lacking in original thought, occasionally come up with an excellent idea.

Although there was never any question of recruiting women for Sabre Squadron service in the SAS, during the mid-1970s the 14th Intelligence and Security Company (DET) began studying the possibilities of employing them permanently on covert operations in Northern Ireland. Following discussions between the Security Service (MI5), the SAS and the army's Intelligence Corps, planners conceived a top secret, controversial, and highly dangerous role for servicewomen which would place them in the front line of the undeclared war against Irish terrorism.

For almost three decades, civil unrest and bloodshed in Ulster, bombings on the mainland and attacks against military personnel in Europe, have been a thorn in the side of successive British governments, and despite countless attempts by well-meaning politicians, and others whose ambitions are more suspect, the savage sectarian feuding drags on. Most of the time the fighting and the bombing is unseen by the public, 'The Troubles' consisting of a newsflash on the radio or a few images on television; but the covert, invisible war that has been waged against Irish terrorists has been one of the most secret operations that British troops have engaged in since the Second World War.

It was, and still is, a struggle fought in the shadows, and it is often misunderstood by those not directly involved in it. Whenever violent incidents did occur in the province they were invariably sudden and without warning, and for many years the gunmen and the bombers seemed to have everything their own way. For those soldiers working on 'special duties' (the term normally given to their undercover activities), there was little room for mistakes. Only those individuals who could be counted on were welcomed by DET and the other undercover units operating in the province. A veteran of many covert operations summed it up like this:

To understand what really happens there [in Northern Ireland] you've got to get into the mind of the gunman and understand the way he thinks, what makes him tick. They're like anyone else, with girlfriends, wives and families, and women have a habit of noticing things that us men fail to see. When you're operating undercover, two or more men in a Q-car are easily noticed, so having a woman along immediately draws less attention. The problem has always been that male operators always considered girls to be a liability in that kind of work because if the shit hits the fan, they wouldn't be able to fight their way out. You've got to understand what you're getting into in a place like Ulster. It's the Wild West, and if you come unstuck you're dead.

When I was first over there it took me a long time to comprehend the mentality of violence on those streets. One night, some Protestant thugs got hold of this Catholic lad and gave him a good kicking just off the Shankill Road. They were all well pissed and then they started stabbing him. Not content with that, one of them got into his car and began running the guy over, going backwards and forwards until he was well and truly 'taity-bread' [dead]. They were about to leave when one of them noticed his Doc Martens [boots] which looked as if they were the same size as his own feet. So this lad goes back, unlaces the boots carefully, and takes them home with him. I ask you, is that the sort of place you'd like your girlfriend or wife to be snooping around in the middle of the night? Most men wouldn't.

The vast majority of people have never personally seen someone shot down in the street or blown up by a bomb and have a tendency to see only the bigger picture. They're looking for a long-term political solution to a conflict that has actually been simmering over there since the Battle of the Boyne in 1690. That's fine, you can understand that deep inbred hatred, and there are people with good intentions there trying to win the hearts and minds of both communities. Good luck to the moderate men and women who believe that the best way to resolve the problem comes from educating and stimulating the younger generation and giving them something to look forward to. But until these people find a way of convincing a seventeen-year-old kid not to join a local gang and pick up an Armalite or an AK-47, it will simply go on and on.

One thing that outsiders fail to understand is the camaraderie and the spirit of adventure amongst gunmen and bombers. They start when they're just kids, nicking a car for the Provos, then progressing to terrorism. To say that they are politically motivated or that they're fighting against British imperialism on their island of Ireland would be an insult to real freedom fighters around the world. Yes, there are idealists on both sides fighting for a cause they believe in, but nearly all the gunmen in PIRA or the UVF, and certainly their families, draw the dole and live off the British state! It's a very personal and family-orientated

144

conflict. Someone who lives in the same street or down the road at the next farm blows themselves to smithereens with a bomb, has half his head taken off with a bullet by the other side, or gets wasted by the security forces. Next thing you know, the bloke's coffin is draped with the Irish tricolour or the Union flag and is being trailed by hundreds of mourners on their slow march to the graveyard. Ninety per cent of them never even knew him, but they're walking behind their hero. You can see the same thing happening all over the world from the Palestinians in the West Bank to the Sicilians in Palermo. It really doesn't matter who the dead warrior was, suddenly he's another martyr for the cause, someone to be avenged by his brothers-in-arms.

You've also got some very private battles going on inside the Provisional IRA, the Irish National Liberation Army, the Ulster Volunteer Force and the Ulster Freedom Fighters (UFF) that are never really understood or talked about in the press. It's the same with all guerrilla groups. Usually their personal discipline is pretty lax, and whatever command structure exists, it's generally founded on fear and a certain admiration for the commanding officer's machismo. Someone recalls the time when Padraig This or Billy That opened fire on his enemy and cut him down with incoming bullets cracking over his head, and you've got yourself a walking, talking legend. You'd see examples of this in Long Kesh [the Maze prison] before they built the H-blocks. It was just like a Second World War POW camp in Germany with all the prisoners locked up in compounds behind the barbed wire. The Long Kesh prisoners received their food parcels, dug their tunnels, distilled their hooch, and carved Kalashnikovs from bits of wood. There would always be some charismatic hero whose sole claim to fame was that he'd blown up Marks

& Spencer's in Royal Avenue or shot three off-duty RUC reservists in the back. That's the reality of guerrilla war, it's not some romantic, poetic fight against evil.

Then they'd have weapon training lectures and learn from the experts about siting and priming culvert bombs to blow up police and army patrols in bandit country. On one of the walls in a Republican 'cage' there was a magnificent painted mural showing the rolling hills of South Armagh, an army patrol coming down the road, and a command wire running up to Paddy and Mick on the hilltop who were waiting to press the plunger and blow the squaddies to hell. It takes quite a bit of courage to initiate an ambush, especially when you're up against a professional army like ours, but perhaps most important is the comradeship.

It's the same in the SAS. There's been a tendency over the years of conflict in Ulster to dismiss the terrorists as a bunch of cut-throats, hooligans and madmen, but then you hear that said about the SAS too. The men pulling the strings inside the proscribed terrorist groups in Ireland today are much more like the Kray twins than Che Guevara. Whether they're Loyalist or Republican, they're cunning, bitter, and utterly ruthless. That's the only way they've managed to survive so long, and they're respected and feared by the people who do their dirty work for them.

Each of the organizations is run like a business with money coming in and going out to buy the beer, and pay the members and the families of dead volunteers and those behind bars. Because the Inland Revenue never sees their books, this means that the money is wild and never properly accounted for. It's gangsterism big-scale, with every nasty little scam you can imagine going on, from protection rackets to prostitution and drugs. Whenever a ceasefire is implemented and they're not shooting or bombing the security forces and each other, they go back to their kangaroo courts, drilling kneecaps with portable Black & Deckers and carrying out punishment killings. Anyone who grew up in the Gorbals [a slum area of Glasgow] in the 1950s or 1960s might get the picture, but for most people it would be like trying to describe the planet Mars to them. Most of us, and you can understand why, were against the idea at the beginning of women working undercover in a place like this.

The establishment of the army's 12th Intelligence and Security Company in Ulster in 1972 was of little interest to most soldiers serving in the province, or for that matter anyone else, but the Intelligence Corps, 'the green slime' to SAS men, had found a very special role in Northern Ireland. During that year Stormont's parliament was dissolved, special category status was introduced for members of terrorist groups, and thirteen demonstrators were shot to death in Londonderry by soldiers from the Parachute Regiment. A spate of no-warning bombs blasted Northern Ireland's city streets and brought pain, suffering and death to hundreds of civilians who were unlucky enough to be in the wrong place at the wrong time.

In that same year however, the army's Intelligence Corps was beginning to find its feet and establish itself quietly in the province. Based at Lisburn army barracks, clerks kept records, analysed information about terrorists and filed documents. Their role appeared on the surface to be simple and rather boring 'admin', but from this apparently humble organization grew greater things. Intelligence and Security companies staffed by members of the Intelligence Corps had existed for some years, especially in Germany where part of their

147

job was to monitor British troops' relationships with German nationals and collate and distribute to soldiers information about Soviet forces and their equipment.

In Ulster, however, their task was to amass information, independently, and store it away from the eyes of the Royal Ulster Constabulary and the Ulster Defence Regiment (now the Royal Irish Regiment). Both organizations, which operated closely with British soldiers, were predominantly Protestant, and there were suspicions during the early days of 'the Troubles' (as there are now) that confidential information about Republican suspects was leaking from the RUC and the UDR to Protestant paramilitary groups. There was also a feeling among security experts in London that Irishmen in general, be they Catholic or Protestant, had a tendency to talk too much, and were not that good at keeping secrets. On numerous occasions carefully laid ambushes against terrorists were compromised, and the only explanation that could be found was that someone, somewhere had talked.

The 14th Intelligence and Security Company,[2] as discussed in the previous chapter, was a completely different kind of organization from the other Intelligence and Security companies, and in early 1974, its new members began their first experimental covert operations. In each of the three army brigades in Northern Ireland, a detachment (or DET) from 14 Int. set up its operations centre, with accommodation for around twenty operators. DET recruits were listed in their army records as being posted to 'special duties' and

[2] In 1974, soldiers serving with 14 Int. were listed as being on secondment to NITAT, the Northern Ireland Training and Advisory Team. The real NITAT trained soldiers in patrolling techniques and booby-trap precautions in England and Germany and these men were being posted to Northern Ireland.

only people who had a real need to know were told what the soldiers were really doing. Before DET's operations began, female army volunteers had occasionally, though rarely, been attached to one of DET's predecessors, the Mobile Reconnaissance Force (MRF, also described earlier) and had taken part in surveillance operations in the province. This only became known when, as has been said, an MRF unit using a Four Square Laundry van as cover was discovered and attacked on 2 October 1972 by PIRA gunmen. The covert mission, designed to spy on suspects in Belfast's Twinbrook Estate and examine and chemically analyse suspected terrorists' clothing and bedding for traces of explosive, had been blown. In the ensuing gun attack, an MRF soldier was shot dead, but his female companion managed to escape by the skin of her teeth.

A damage-control exercise by Intelligence planners was put into operation. It was decided that adverse publicity surrounding the death or capture of female soldiers would be counter-productive to the success of Northern Ireland operations. Such unsavoury incidents would, it was said, produced an outcry from the British public, but probably give PIRA a valuable media coup.

Of course, any PIRA assassin responsible for killing a woman operative would be pilloried in the world's press, but those in charge of covert operations at the time considered the place for female soldiers to be either behind a desk with a typewriter, or running the telephone switchboard. Women were certainly not to be allowed to patrol Belfast and Derry streets carrying guns like the men. It was, they decided, simply too dangerous. The fact that this decision was taken by men is, of course, another matter. To say that the decision to use female operators again was taken only when the worst of the Troubles were over, would be doing an injustice to the courage that these very special women showed in their dangerous operations, and following the attack on the Four Square Laundry van, women, especially from the RUC, did still take part in occasional covert operations. Several years passed before the intelligence-gathering organizations in Northern Ireland 'got their act together' under the control of the Tasking and Co-Ordination Group (TCG), and it was only then that the Security Service (MI5) hierarchy saw a specific role for women which could not under any circumstances be played by men.

The world, even in the shady business of undercover operations, was changing. During the latter part of the 1970s and early 1980s in Britain, women finally began to establish themselves in positions of political and economic power. Margaret Thatcher was the country's authoritarian Prime Minister, and at MI5, Stella Rimington was pursuing a dynamic career which resulted in her becoming that agency's first woman director. The Security Service had won the long-running battle against their colleagues at the Secret Intelligence Service (MI6), and had swallowed up Ulster in the fight against terrorism, leaving the 'old school-tie brigade' (as some people saw them) in SIS to get on with their traditional job of watching and influencing the rest of the world.

Many SIS employees, it must be said, were quite happy to accept this *fait accompli* and were delighted to be posted to the Tropics instead of taking the shuttle to Belfast. On the European mainland, the Security Service was developing important contacts within the EC's internal security agencies, liaising with anti-terrorist forces and exchanging information on terrorists groups. Before long, much of Western Europe and even places further east would fall under their area of operations in the counter-terrorist war.

To most British soldiers, the idea that females could withstand the rigours of the battlefield or that they could possess the sheer stamina required to keep up with their male counterparts has always been dismissed out of hand. Comments like, 'It's not in a woman's nature to wage war', or 'They simply haven't got the physical strength', are common in military barracks throughout the world whenever the subject arises. Sending women into perilous war zones to carry out covert operations was not, however, a new idea. During the Second World War the Special Operations Executive (SOE) and its American equivalent, the Office of Strategic Services (OSS) recognized the potential of women agents in behind-the-lines operations and recruited foreign-language speakers for insertion into Nazi-occupied Europe. Selection procedures were severely rigorous, for as well as requiring great courage, women agents had to be able to defend themselves while operating in constant fear for their lives. Their ability to withstand physical and mental hardship was proven repeatedly despite the almost suicidal capture rate which faced them. Many perished at the hands of their Gestapo torturers, faced firing squads or died of malnutrition and disease in German extermination camps, but still they volunteered. There are well-documented accounts of women surviving in hostile conditions where their male colleagues have died, but most importantly, and especially in Northern Ireland, women were often less likely to draw attention to themselves than men. Unless you have attended an intensive counter-terrorist course, you are unlikely to expect a woman to be carrying a gun or planting a bomb. Veterans of guerrilla wars in South-East Asia, Central America and Algeria knew better. They learnt quickly to beware of highly motivated females who were prepared to carry out acts of terror while their menfolk were being watched or searched by the security forces:

> When Harold Wilson announced in 1974 that the SAS were being deployed to South Armagh, the IRA and everyone else put two and two together and made five. Whenever a gunman got shot by the security forces they all said 'The SAS did it' and the fact is, it rarely was. Rumours started spreading about what SAS men looked like as they prowled around the streets looking for wanted terrorists, and the general assumption was that we all had long hair, shaggy beards and sneaked around dressed in torn jeans with patches on our backsides and donkey jackets with 'Wimpey' written on the back. They also assumed we'd be driving a bashed-up Ford Cortina with the headlights smashed or hanging off, just like some of the boyos from the Creggan or the Bogside [Republican areas of Londonderry]. The people who were most at risk were undercover operators who fitted the stereotype image in the heads of the opposition. That's why women in DET were so effective. Your average gunman doesn't expect to be eyeballed by a young lass buying a pint of milk in the corner shop. Many of our ideas in the early days came from the USA and their drug-enforcement people. You have to be able to fit into the landscape and simply not be noticed.

In a nutshell and as the MoD, MI5 and the SAS soon found out, women can make extremely covert operators, and when armed, they can be just as deadly as their male counterparts.

By the early 1980s, 14th Intelligence and Security Company had established itself alongside the RUC's Mobile Support Units and Special Branch's E4 and E4A as perhaps the most effective counter-terrorist unit in the province. E4A was in fact created by the RUC when they saw how effective DET had become. Again, as has been said, several of 14 Int.'s members had served in the Regiment, and others would later go on to pass SAS selection. Some of those who went from DET to Hereford and won their SAS berets returned later in their careers with their squadrons to Northern Ireland, or became members of the Ulster-dedicated SAS Troop. Intensive training had given DET operators not only the ability to carry out close-observation activities against suspected terrorists in hostile areas, but also the ability to engage and beat them with firearms if they offered resistance to arrest. Although initially DET personnel rarely stayed more than a few months in Northern Ireland, this did offer them a certain anonymity and reduced to some extent the risks of them being 'sussed' by their enemies. As one ex-member explained.

> If we'd stayed any longer the boyos [terrorists] would have started to know our faces like some of the Special Branch guys who live permanently over there. They're exposed to the threat of assassination 24 hours a day, 365 days a year.

The SAS's specially designed DET selection course had been created to select men and not women, but when it was suggested to Training Wing in Hereford that they might be sent a few female candidates, the Regiment's tough NCOs were intrigued. Why not, some asked, try them out and see how far they got? At worst, women candidates would fail the tests and simply be returned to their original units. On the other hand one or two might pass, and this could open up a useful new area of undercover work in the province. Recruitment of women into DET drew candidates not only from the army but from all branches of the armed forces including the (now disbanded) Women's Royal Naval Service (the Wrens).

The selection programme, run by members of the SAS's B Squadron and the Training Wing NCOs, was based on the same criteria as the men's, with candidates being forced to complete a series of physical-fitness tests and rigorous cross-country endurance exercises over the Welsh mountains carrying a heavy bergen and using map and compass for navigation. They were also examined by a group of counter-terrorist experts whose job was to analyse the recruit's character for stamina, intelligence, her powers of observation and memory. A forty-eight-hour 'Joint Arms' resistance to interrogation test based on the SAS's own selection programme rounded off the process, with the women being subjected to strip-searches, gruelling interrogations and sleep deprivation. Standing tied and blindfolded in a rain-swept farmyard at night, with cars driving around you at high speed is enough to make most people crack and throw in their hand.

As with SAS selection, many applied for the jobs but only a few passed. Those that succeeded were cautiously welcomed into the previously all-male Hereford garrison at Stirling Lines, where the men who had 'pushed them to hell and back' during selection now had a chance to get to know them socially. Invitations to the Regiment's mess and the notorious Paludrine Club resulted in some intensive drinking, and the women who had displayed their physical and mental strength during selection now showed the men that they could hold their own with a glass in their hand at the bar. As frequently happens when SAS men get together and alcohol flows freely, some of the drinking sessions degenerated into loud and violent games, of the sort common in a rugby club or during a stag night, but rarely witnessed by women. At least one new female DET member entered into the spirit of the occasion and joined in with wild abandon, shocking some extremely hard-nosed veterans and leaving several lost for words. Not only, it seemed, were DET's new recruits capable of lugging heavy bergens over long distances on rain- and wind-blown mountains like their colleagues in the Regiment, some had an amazing capacity for alcohol too.

So what kind of woman was determined enough, or some would say foolhardy enough, to want to join DET? The physical requirements to begin with were severe, so only those with stamina and athletic fitness were chosen. Most of them were in their mid-twenties and had already served several years in the forces. Their ability to 'think fast on their feet' was the next priority, coupled with a higher than normal IQ, an excellent memory and a solid determination to succeed. Suggestions by some who met them that they were 'tomboys' were somewhat unfair, for in makeup and lipstick, high heels and a slinky evening gown they would certainly make most men's heads turn. This led to interesting and sometimes romantic reactions from SAS men who encountered them. There were some fairly predictable chat-up scenarios, usually handled skilfully by the women themselves, and a fair amount of chivalrous behaviour from officers and other ranks who occasionally came to their rescue if things got out of hand.

The women's training programme was taken very seriously by all the new recruits, and predictably, most soon became crack shots with the Browning Hi-Power pistol, the Heckler & Koch MP5-K, the pump-action shotgun and a number of other weapons. By the time they were ready to go to Ulster their marksmanship would reach a quite phenomenal level. Several also pursued, with a certain passion, the basic unarmed-combat training that was taught to them. Not content with learning restraining and self-defence techniques which are learned by most policemen for making arrests, several began using the *kubotan* like their male DET and SAS colleagues and became seriously interested in the martial arts. Judo, ju-jitsu, kung fu, tai-kwan-do and other lesser-known, if equally violent, adaptations of bar-room combat and street fighting were enthusiastically added to their repertory. Their eager instructors were some of the SAS's toughest soldiers, delighted to meet women who were prepared to take them on in the gym. The reader will perhaps naturally assume that these SAS unarmed-combat instructors went softly on their female students, but apparently this was not the case. These intensive training sessions, by accident rather than design, were turning 14 Intelligence Company's 'secret weapons' into an extraordinarily effective fighting force It still remained to be seen, however, whether these carefully selected women would stand up to the pressure of actual operations. Opinions among the men who were involved in their training about a woman's suitability for undercover operations varied, and some had strong feelings:

If you ask most squaddies what they think about women in uniform the answer is usually the same, they're either really ugly, or they're dykes and hate men, or they're nurses. If they're nurses, they're always real stunners, good-looking chicks, or at least that's the myth. No one really knows where this idea comes from, least of all the ordinary soldier, but that's the sort of everyday comment that gets said. Of course it's completely ridiculous and the reason is probably that WRACs and WRENs [Women's Royal Army Corps and Women's Royal Naval Service] are doing the same jobs, more or less, as the men, so this doesn't leave them much time for frat-ernization. They see each other in a rather dull uniform most of the time, and frankly, a girl in a green woolly, OGs, [olive-green army trousers] and boots isn't that sexy. The other thing is that if a bloke tries it on with one of them and he doesn't score all his mates find out and he'll sometimes call her a dyke out of sheer frustration because he's been rejected. It's probably just a way of covering himself. That doesn't of course stop a lot of guys from trying though, especially after a few bevvies.

When the first DET woman arrived in Northern Ireland they had already received training in many of the specialized techniques used today in modern undercover operations. These included the use of concealed communications systems in a vehicle or hidden in clothing, exercises where 'suspects', usually played by the instructors, were tailed, with several operators working in teams and switching places to reduce the risk of compromise, and fast, tactical driving. The latter would impress most rally drivers. Students were taught to drive 'on the edge' of safety limits, and usually very, very fast. The Highway Code and normal rules of the road were thrown out of the window, and cars with highly tuned engines simply became machines to be pushed to the limits, machines which, like a handgun, might one day save their lives in an ambush. Travelling on country lanes at speeds which would petrify most experienced traffic policemen, overtaking on blind corners, and carrying out handbrake turns in clouds of dust and burning rubber became routine driving skills that terrorized all but the coolest of passengers.

Learning to handle hi-tech camera equipment with 'see-in-the-dark' or black-light capabilities ('black light' is the electromagnetic radiation in the infrared and ultraviolet ends of the spectrum), which included still cameras and video systems, was another skill which had to be learned and properly understood, as also was the use of 'bugs', tiny microphones and tracking devices. With some of the latest hi-tech bugs, they were told, it was possible to track a person, weapon or vehicle without compromising an operator who before such things were invented, would have had physically to follow a suspect.

They learned about 'jarking', which during the early days of the conflict in Northern Ireland was a slang word for tampering with a terrorist gun or bomb to make it explode when it was used. Such practices, although quite common in most other guerrilla wars, were firmly outlawed by the British Army in Northern Ireland, despite allegations to the contrary from some Republicans. There have often been protests from British soldiers who consider that booby-trapping your enemy's arms caches is a perfectly reasonable and legitimate technique to use against ruthless terrorists but, officially anyway, it has never been allowed. Jarking in army parlance today means implanting a homing device, in such a way that it should not be detected by a terrorist, in a weapon usually found in a terrorist cache, so that its movement can be monitored.

Other highly sophisticated and very secret equipment which is used in today's counter-terrorist wars was demonstrated to the DET women, some of it so revolutionary in its capabilities that it made James Bond's boffin, 'Q', look like a nineteenth-century scientist. Whatever gadgetry government scientists came up with, they were told, at the end of the day the individual operator was of much more value. This was much the same as had applied to the Spitfires and Hurricanes in the Second World War; they were easy enough to build, but to train a pilot took months of hard work. The operator would always be more important than the equipment, and if circumstances dictated that they should smash their way through a hostile roadblock, thereby half-wrecking their car, then that's what they should do. Any obstacle, if it could not be gently and passively negotiated, should be demolished in order to gain access to the other side. This applied to fences, doors, and any other barrier which might impede their free movement. Gradually the DET women were learning about controlled aggression, how to rein it in and how to release it with tremendous, unstoppable violence. The Regiment trains its troopers to burst into a room and attack a target, either an object or a human being, with their bare hands.

> One man stormed in and smashed the punchbag so violently he broke his wrist with one blow . . . it's got to be the most violently aggressive act you've ever performed, you give it everything, either with your bare hands, an iron bar or weapon, it doesn't matter how you do it, you just fight through until you've won. That's something that can be taught if you've got the right human material. Women in general have this ability just like men, but you have to encourage them and bring it to the surface.

When the first of the now fully trained women finally arrived in Northern Ireland and were given a tour of some of the better known danger zones in the province, there was a certain reluctance among several of the men to work with them. It would take some time before this attitude started to change. They attended briefings given by RUC Special Branch officers and members of the Security Service who outlined the latest 'state of play' in the province and briefed them on known terrorists and their activities. The amount of information held by the SB in Northern Ireland and stored on the army's own computers was quite phenomenal. Not only did they keep databases about each individual terrorist in the finest detail, their habits and personal relationships with wives, girlfriends and one another were also carefully documented. Vehicles could be traced and identified in seconds not only from their registration ('index') numbers, but also from engine serial numbers. This was the heart of the secret war being fought against terrorism in Northern Ireland and on the British mainland, a meticulously collated intelligence-gathering machine that has been developed over almost thirty years.

The task of DET operators was to feed that machine with up-to-the-minute information and be prepared to deal with bombers and gunmen as they prepared their terrorist acts. If a particular threat appeared too great for DET personnel to handle, the SAS was on call to back them up. Many of their tasks would involve them working closely with one of the army Tasking and Co-ordination Group liaison officers, who was usually a middle-ranking captain or major with SAS experience. Accommodated in grim Portakabins located inside security force bases with very few of the comforts of home, some of the women must have wondered what they had let themselves in for.

The job they were there to do would bring them into close contact with some of Northern Ireland's most dangerous terrorists, and several of their DET predecessors had already given their lives on operations. The first of them to die was Captain Tony Pollen. On 14 April 1974, while attached to the Londonderry-based DET unit, Captain Pollen and another plain-clothes soldier were working undercover and taking photographs of a Republican demonstration. At some point, the two men attracted the attention of some of the protesters, which is not a difficult thing to do in Londonderry's Bogside. Within seconds, Pollen lay dead, gunned down in the street, though his companion, by dint of quick reactions, managed to break clear and escape.

This was followed on 14 December 1977 by the murder of another DET operator when Corporal Paul Harman, who was engaged in undercover work and driving a red Morris Marina, was surrounded by a hostile crowd on the Monagh Road in Belfast's Turf Lodge Estate. His body was later discovered in the wreckage of his burnt-out car. The corporal had been shot in the back and head, and his Browning pistol had gone.

Most of DET's work, for both the men and the women, involved targeting individual terrorist suspects, watching them from makeshift hides, derelict buildings or undercover Q-cars, and building up a detailed picture of their habits and lifestyles. Getting into position was undoubtedly the most difficult aspect of this work – getting out was something that could be thought about later. As a rule, operators on covert 'Obbo' (observation) work carried out their tasks in pairs, with another pair of DET or SAS soldiers close by. Even with this precaution, however, things could still go terribly wrong.

In February 1984, two DET soldiers were tasked to set up a covert OP overlooking the home of twenty-one-year-old Henry Hogan, whom Special Branch believed to be a prominent member of PIRA's North Antrim active service unit. The two DET operators chose the site for their hide, which presented technical problems as Hogan's house was in a cul-de-sac with little good cover nearby. The site they chose was in a field behind a fence. Beside them was a telegraph pole, and nearby some workmen's huts. Their OP was about seventy-five metres away from their target's front door. As is usual with this kind of operation, they chose to insert themselves after dark, approaching the OP from the rear by crossing a field. Carrying out such a delicate and dangerous manoeuvre is far from easy, and the DET team had not taken into account the presence of a powerful street light nearby. It is believed that someone noticed movement as the team either approached their hide or once they were in it, but either way, their mission was compromised. At about eight o'clock on the night of 21 February, a number of PIRA gunmen approached the soldiers' position, using the same route that the DET team themselves had taken. There was a loud burst of gunfire, and as the PIRA unit made off across a field, twenty-six-year-old Sergeant Paul Oram lay dead, and his companion seriously wounded. The soldiers' backup team (three DET operators) arrived in two Ford Cortinas, within what some eye-witnesses said was seconds of the initial bursts of gunfire, and then more shots were heard. When the firing stopped, two PIRA gunmen, Declan Dominic Peter Martin, aged eighteen, and Henry John Hogan, whose house DET had been watching, were also dead. The army Quick-Reaction Force (QRF) which arrived on the scene a few minutes later found the PIRA men's weapons, an Armalite and a 9mm Vigneron sub-machine gun.

In fact, Hogan knew he was under surveillance. During the days before the shooting the PIRA gunman had suspected that he was being followed. On a trip to Maghera and Draperstown with some friends, he had stopped his car and had noticed another car behind him also stop. This happened on two occasions. That was enough for Hogan, who was now certain he was the subject of a security forces investigation. When movement was spotted near his home he and two other men left the back of his house and doubled round behind the DET operators. Suddenly a blue Mini pulled up at Hogan's house. At the same moment, and probably distracted by the car, the three PIRA gunmen confronted the two soldiers with a shouted challenge. Sergeant Oram and his companion swung round and found themselves facing three armed men. There was a pause, then both soldiers went for their Browning Hi-Power pistols. In the fierce gun battle that followed, and which lasted only a few, violent seconds, four of the five men involved were hit. The third PIRA gunman, who had been carrying a shotgun, escaped. This then, was the reality of undercover work in Ulster, and DET women were now a part of it.

Tip-offs about forthcoming bombings, shootings or arms caches nearly always came from human sources (HUMINT) rather than from tape-recorded telephone intercepts or hidden microphones. Although some of these hi-tech devices were useful for checking information, the old-fashioned informer or 'copper's nark' was still the most useful source of terrorist intelligence. As the women began work on the city streets and in the rural areas,[3] they were initially always teamed-up with at least one male DET operator or a member of the SAS's small, permanent Northern Ireland troop.

They gradually began to discover the intricate and painstaking business of covert surveillance, never getting too close to the targeted suspects, their homes or their haunts. The job required patience, alertness and close attention to fine detail. It also needed, as one ex-SAS trooper put it, 'lots of bottle'. There was no reason to draw attention to oneself. Modern technology in the form of easily concealable video cameras often fitted with fibre-optic lenses could be placed to watch suspect locations, reducing the risk of compromise. But as with all modern hi-tech devices, they work marvellously

[3] Originally most DET operations took place in country areas, leaving RUC's E4 and E4A to operate in the cities, but this changed from 1980 onwards when DET were frequently deployed in both rural and urban environments.

until something goes wrong. Abysmal weather conditions could reduce visibility, and electrical systems did not always work as well as they should.

Video tapes could be carefully analysed later in the safety of security force bases, but first the spy cameras had to be put into position, usually in the heart of a hardline Republican stronghold where the eyes and ears of potential assassins were as closely focused and highly tuned as those of a pack of angry Doberman guard dogs. Any stranger seen entering such territory without good reason would be quickly 'eyeballed' by the opposition, and women, children and family pets were often the first to sound the alarm.

All kinds of ingenious methods were used to insert operators into these areas, and this required a fleet of specially equipped vehicles, often the more battered the better, which would not look out of place. Sometimes though, this 'old-banger-look-as-rough-as-possible' technique literally backfired on the operators, and actually drew attention to them. Engines were finely tuned for speed, and both the registration numbers and the cars themselves were frequently changed. 'Off-hands' communications were fitted enabling drivers to talk to their bases and their colleagues in other vehicles without using a telltale handset. Some cunning disguises and props which would have impressed the finest character actors on a London stage were used, and all DET team members, when away from their vehicles, were equipped with a concealed state-of-the-art two-way radio, with microphones hidden in their collars and discreet earpieces. To transmit, the operator had simply to touch a pressel switch, usually fastened to the wrist.

Driving or walking around hardline Republican or Loyalist areas wearing this kit required great courage from DET operators, male and female, and each of them quickly learned the meaning of 'the adrenalin rush'. This would occur each time they were in hostile territory and their cover looked as if it were about to be blown. Even though they were always armed with a concealed handgun, usually a Browning Hi-Power with a 20-round magazine or a Sig Sauer, and sometimes a Heckler & Koch MP5-K with twin 30-round mags, discovery would leave them with very little chance of escaping with their lives from an angry crowd.

> Probably the most feared situation, the one nightmares are made of, is not in fact coming face to face with one or two or more PIRA gunmen in a firefight situation, but rather when you get trapped in a car. You're in a tin box, and unless there's a way of driving through the danger, you're probably in for a slow and very nasty death. The chances are, as happened with Bob Nairac (see p. 132), they're going to torture you first. The idea of keeping a spare round for yourself did occur once or twice, but it wasn't really something you'd waste too much time thinking or talking about.

A frightening example of what can happen occurred in 1988 when two soldiers in civilian clothes, Corporals Robert Howes and Derek Wood, who had nothing to do with undercover operations in the province, accidentally drove into a PIRA funeral cortege in West Belfast. The gory details of what occurred next were witnessed by millions of television viewers all around the world. Unable to drive out of the traffic jam and blocked in by other vehicles, their car was quickly surrounded. A frenzied mob, believing the two men to be either Loyalist gunmen or undercover soldiers, then launched a frenzied, murderous attack, smashing the car's windows and grabbing inside at Corporals Howes and Wood. Just before being overpowered and with

165

nowhere to run, television viewers saw one of the doomed men brandishing a Browning Hi-Power pistol with a standard 13-round magazine, but apart from firing one shot, apparently in the air, he seemed to make little attempt to defend himself with it. It was clear from their predicament that they had not been trained to cope with such a scenario.

With the mob smashing their way into the car, the two soldiers were quickly overpowered and dragged away to face a merciless beating. Then, having suffered injuries that left them virtually unrecognizable, they were driven to waste ground near by and shot dead. Claims by Republican activists that the corporals belonged to a secret British undercover unit were quickly dismissed by the Ministry of Defence and the RUC – with good reason, for had they been members of the SAS or DET, it is unlikely the mob would have had things quite so much their own way. Most special forces soldiers, in similar circumstances, realizing the gravity of the situation and recognizing that their lives were in imminent danger, would have opened fire without hesitation and fought their way out of the trap. If unsuccessful, they would at least have died trying.

Corporals Howes and Wood were in fact ordinary British Army signallers engaged on a normal changeover of personnel, one of the pair having just finished his tour in Northern Ireland and the other having arrived to take his place. The result of their innocent but misguided sightseeing tour of Belfast clearly demonstrated the constant danger to British soldiers on that city's streets, a lesson carefully studied by the covert operators who worked in those neighbourhoods.

From the mid 1970s until the spring of 1980, the SAS had been deployed to Ulster in squadron strength of around sixty men in the three operational areas throughout the province. After that, the Northern Ireland-dedicated SAS troop was formed and worked in conjunction with three separate DET groups, each with its own area of responsibility. With the TCG now collating and acting on information supplied by MI5's HUMINT, SIGINT and ELINT (electronic intelligence) sources, and with an extremely capable and courageous band of soldiers, both men and women, working on the ground, the overall picture began to change for the better.

DET's undercover women carried out their operations in both town and country, often pairing up with one of the men and passing themselves off as a courting couple, a sight not unusual in quiet rural lanes or on a city's park benches. Covert operations in strife-torn Ulster had changed dramatically. One or two male DET operators now began thoroughly to enjoy some of their dangerous assignments, for what could be more ordinary and pleasurable than a boy and a girl walking down a city street together, or sitting in a pub laughing and joking? One of the greatest problems facing all DET's operators, however, was their accents. Most, after a short period of tuition, could mimic a few Northern Irish phrases without their true, normally English origins being identified, but for safety, 'English' conversation was kept to a minimum. The fact that some DET personnel were of Irish origin helped such situations enormously.

Morale among the men noticeably improved, and with that came a mixture of admiration for DET women and a predictable masculine desire to protect them. A gallant or sympathetic gesture would often be rejected, however, leading to some friction between male and female personnel. Relationships developed which would have fascinated and perhaps mystified most psychologists and women's liberationists. This resulted in some frenzied sexual relationships between special forces men and women which are perhaps better left to the memories of the participants rather than being described by this author. Suffice it to say that at least one DET woman soldier decided it was in the interest of her job to get 'matters of the flesh' over and done with so that she and her male partner could get back to work.

Formal accusations of sexual harassment were rare (most female operators being quite capable of defending themselves against men), and were normally resolved quietly and without resort to an authority higher than the unit's commanding officer, whose task, it has to be said, was an extremely difficult one. Not only did that job require sensitivity, it also demanded the patience of a saint and the strength of a lion, with an excellent understanding of human nature thrown in for good measure, for the people under his command all had extremely strong temperaments. The commander's first and most fundamental priority was to ensure the safety of the operators, and anything that might jeopardize their lives had to be resolved decisively and without prejudice. If this meant separating the members of a team whose characters clashed for some reason, or returning an operator to his or her original unit for no apparent reason, this was done without long explanations or delay. Professional male soldiers have little time for feeble excuses, most especially when they come from women who are doing essentially the same job as themselves. Jokes in poor taste about such-and-such a DET woman being a bit 'off-colour today' because she was 'suffering from PMT' (pre-menstrual tension), or had not had a 'good rogering' for ages, were common, extremely hurtful, and had to be dealt with as a matter of routine. How the women coped with this is unclear, and the inner resources they drew on are impressive. They were operating in a predominantly male environment, surrounded by hostile mobs that would delight in killing them, but cope they did. In the final analysis these intrepid women fighters drove cars just as skilfully, fired their guns just as accurately, and took the same risks as the men. The vast majority of men who served with them on operations admit today that the preconceived opinions most of them had about their female colleagues were misguided.

The effect on terrorist suspects when suddenly confronted by one of these charming and heavily armed young women was simply mind-boggling, and the gunmen and bombers who were intercepted by them undoubtedly suffered the biggest shock of their lives. Closing in on their target in the classic, double-handed pistol-firing position, or brandishing an MP5-K submachine gun while screaming 'Freeze! Army!', was enough to make most people stop dead in their tracks or faint with the shock. One quick glance told the individual at the wrong end of the gun barrel that the weapon's owner meant business. Those carrying arms in a threatening manner rarely had the time to consider their predicament or study their opponent, and usually died where they stood.

DET women took part in many of the successful operations against Republican and Loyalist terrorists during the late 1980s and 1990s, including several of the SAS's most accomplished and best publicized Northern Ireland coups. Acting as the eyes and ears of the Regiment, they became highly accomplished at recceing areas where the presence of male operators would have been noticed, and where backup from other members of the security forces was often several life-threatening minutes away. One of the most common tasks was the basic, yet to most people petrifying, 'walk-by'. This consisted simply of going and having a look at a vehicle, house, or the drinkers in a pub. Having spent hours studying the faces of suspected and wanted terrorists in often rather muzzy photographs or on video, they would try to spot a face in a crowd. This would rarely be accomplished the first time round, and the operator was frequently obliged to return, sometimes several times to make sure. Going back to the same area was always one of the most dangerous tasks DET women faced, but they did so often, calling on their reserves of courage and without thinking twice. Knowing that other members of the unit were monitoring their movements was undoubtedly reassuring, but as has been seen in the case of Sergeant Oram, a lot can happen before a backup team arrives.

As with all things military, each operation was given a codename and followed a set of well-established rules. Briefings could be long and detailed affairs behind closed doors with an extraordinary amount of information being studied and discussed. Suspected or known terrorists would be targeted, and over the course of days and often weeks, their private lives would be placed under DET's microscope. Gradually a picture would be built up of the target or targets, the details of their personal lives and their computerized records, if any existed, would be analysed, and slowly DET operators would begin to 'know' them. It was a very odd situation to be in, and the temptation for an operator, on seeing a target in the flesh, to wave and shout 'Hallo! How's the girlfriend?' was at times a difficult one to resist. To say that operators grew to hate the people they spied on would be unjust, for most took their work very seriously and had the same unbiased attitude as the best murder squad detectives. What was important was to catch the criminal, not waste your time thinking about what a nasty character he or she was. But there were certainly occasions when the more an operator learned about his or her target, the more they grew to despise them. Knowing that someone you are watching drink and laugh in a pub has planted a bomb, indiscriminately killing and maiming innocent people, or has murdered a soldier just like you, can produce emotions that will sometimes result in hatred.

In spite of the impressive arrest rate of terrorists and their accomplices in Northern Ireland, many soldiers and policemen serving there consider that prison sentences are either too short or simply ineffective. When a convicted gunman is released from the Maze prison after serving, say, ten years behind bars, and is then discovered to be involved again in terrorist activities, he is very closely monitored, some would say harassed, by the security forces. The rules governing covert operations in Ulster are strict, and while the use of firearms is permitted in exceptional circumstances, DET operators and the SAS cannot engage a target with firearms unless their lives or the lives of others are in immediate danger. This means simply that for a terrorist to be killed, he or she must be caught in the act with a finger on the trigger or preparing to detonate a bomb. Whether this actually happens every time an ambush is mounted is open to conjecture, and there will always be allegations of warnings not being given or of a *coup de grâce* being administered to a captured or wounded gunman. Because there are hardly ever reliable independent witnesses around when these operations take place (as was also the case with accusations against British paratroopers that they had executed Argentine prisoners during the Falklands campaign) it is sometimes impossible to know what really happened.

Covert surveillance operations will often run for months until intelligence leads to cast-iron proof that a terrorist attack is about to take place. When this happens, the full force of DET and the SAS are deployed on operations which will sometimes involve weeks of waiting and disrupted sleep patterns. When an ambush does take place, and shots are fired and terrorists killed, there is a hectic rush to remove the special forces soldiers from the immediate area, usually involving members of the Quick Reaction Force, who have been tasked to secure the perimeter. The elation amongst SAS and DET personnel after a 'successful kill' usually results in a winding-down rest period, and after intense debriefings and the taking of statements, most end up with a large alcoholic drink in their hands. Few covert operators are able to stand such a stressful lifestyle for long and move on to other duties in other military units after a couple of years, though there are cases of DET and Troop (SAS) members returning several times for repeated tours of duty in the province. What on earth make them want to go back?

It's a bit like smoking. On Monday you decide to give up, then at midnight you light up again. It gets into your system and before you know it, you can't live without it. There's also a great social life over there [Northern Ireland] and most of us had very good friends in RUC Special Branch and as they say, 'the crack[4] is excellent'. Of course, the risks are always there and people do get killed, but someone's got to keep the lid on the situation over there. It's a rewarding job, simple as that.

[4] Crack – a chiefly Irish colloquialism for having a good time; fun.

EIGHT

OPERATION FLAVIUS – GIBRALTAR

On 6 March 1988 the SAS, acting on information supplied by MI5, shot dead three members of a PIRA active service unit in Gibraltar. For the members of the Regiment's team that carried out Operation 'Flavius',[1] the events of that day were a clear success. In the eyes of the SAS's critics however, and indeed in the recent opinion of the European Court of Human Rights, Flavius brought about the unlawful killing of three unarmed civilians.

The undisputed facts of the case are that Mairead Farrell, Danny McCann and Sean Savage were, in 1988, members of a PIRA unit when they went to Spain, and from there to Gibraltar, with the intention of planting a bomb to blow up the band of the Royal Anglian Regiment, which was stationed there at the time.

The operation was conceived in the autumn of 1987 in response to the failed attack on Loughgall RUC barracks which had resulted in the deaths of eight PIRA members from the East Tyrone Brigade (see Operation

[1] Gaius Flavius was a fourth-century Roman politician who established the laws of the Roman Empire.

'Judy', Chapter Six). As so often happens with special forces operations, the SAS were called in at almost the last moment to confront the terrorists, although for several weeks MI5 and RUC Special Branch had been aware of a planned attack through HUMINT and SIGINT sources. The piecing together of information by MI5 that led to the deployment of members of the CRW team to Gibraltar was a clear result of the long and painstaking secret war being waged by the Intelligence organizations in Northern Ireland.

The fact is, however, that their information was incomplete, and on 6 March, the SAS were deployed to face three extremely dangerous terrorists who it was believed were planning to detonate their bomb that day with a remote-control triggering device.

The history of the three PIRA members who were to die that day in Gibraltar is in itself an insight into the nature of that organization. Daniel McCann, aged thirty, came from Clonard on the Lower Falls Road in West Belfast. He was eighteen when the Troubles began, and when he was twenty-six and working at the Royal Victoria Hospital, McCann was jailed for six months for taking part in a riot. In that year, 1973, he became a member of PIRA. In January 1979 he was again arrested and sentenced to two years' imprisonment for possessing a detonator. During this sentence in the notorious H-blocks at the Maze prison, he took part in the 'dirty Protest' in which prisoners refused to wash and smeared the walls of their cells with excrement. He was released in January 1981 but re-arrested four months later for possession of a gun. He spent four months on remand, was re-arrested in November and spent a year in jail.

McCann was picked up again in July 1982, but released without charge. Amnesty International, in its report on interrogation procedures at Castlereagh

RUC station, referred to McCann as having been 'ill-treated at Castlereagh interrogation centre'.

Following his death in Gibraltar, *An Phoblact* said, 'He was a life-long activist. He knew no compromise and was to die as he had lived in implacable opposition to Britain's criminal presence in our land.' McCann was also an expert with explosives and triggering devices.

Twenty-three-year-old Sean Savage, the second member of the PIRA team, was a keen amateur cyclist, a non-smoker and non-drinker, and played Gaelic football. Known to his friends as an enthusiastic Irish-language speaker, he had only once been in trouble with the police, in 1982, when he was arrested following information from an informer. There was insufficient evidence to charge him with a crime, and he was released a month later.

Mairead Farrell, aged thirty-one, was convicted in 1976 of planting a bomb at the Conway Hotel in Belfast. Her PIRA companions in that attack were Kieran Doherty and Sean McDermot. McDermot was shot dead by the RUC during that attack, and Doherty died in 1981 while on hunger strike in the Maze prison. In December 1980, Farrell joined the hunger strike protest in Armagh jail, but survived, and in September 1986 she was released. She then went to Queen's University in Belfast, where she studied Politics and Economics. According to friends in Sinn Féin, 'she reported back to the IRA. Her ten and a half years in prison had strengthened her resolve.'

Savage was in Spain in the autumn of 1987, and through the simple interception by British Intelligence of a postcard he sent to his home in Belfast, the counter-terrorist forces decided to keep a watchful eye on him. According to the postcard, he was working on the Costa Brava, and through the ever-increasing co-operation between European anti-terrorist units, the Spanish authorities were made aware of his background and Britain's interest in his activities.

On 15 November a certain Robert Reilly and Brendan Coyne were observed by Spanish authorities transiting through Madrid airport en route between Málaga and Dublin. Spanish Immigration identified the passport photographs of these two men as being those of Sean Savage and Daniel McCann. The passports were false, and this information was passed through to the Servicios de Información bureau in Madrid, and then on to Scotland Yard. During the next four months before the planned attack, MI5 carefully monitored their HUMINT and SIGINT sources, and it was not long before they noticed the activities of an Irishwoman named 'Mary Parkin' in Gibraltar. A careful check of missing and stolen passports came up with some more valuable information. Mary Parkin, the wife of a Press Association journalist, had reported her passport stolen. Whoever was using it was travelling on false papers. The woman had made two trips to Gibraltar, both on Tuesday mornings. On 23 February 1988 she was observed by a team from MI5 watching the changing of the guard ceremony there. On 1 March she was again observed at the guard-changing – on both occasions she followed the route taken by the bandsmen of the Royal Anglian Regiment.

On 2 March the Joint Intelligence Committee (JIC) met in Whitehall, and its members became convinced that a terrorist attack in the dependency was imminent. They passed their information to the Joint Operations Centre (JOC) which is staffed by personnel from MI5, the Ministry of Defence and an SAS liaison officer. There was now a clear belief in Whitehall that PIRA was planning a serious attack in Gibraltar, and it was the job of the JOC to prevent that from happening. A troop of SAS men from the CRW team were placed on alert, and on Thursday, 3 March a seven-man squad flew to Gibraltar. Consisting of a team commander, a second-in-command, four other ranks and an ATO,[2] they quickly linked up with the 'Snuffbox'[3] group that was already in position there.

The CRW team leader was issued with a copy of a document setting out the rules of engagement:

RULES OF ENGAGEMENT FOR THE MILITARY COMMANDER IN OPERATION FLAVIUS

1. These instructions are for your guidance, once your participation in Operation Flavius has been duly authorized.
2. You are to operate as directed by the Gibraltar Police Commissioner or by the officers designated by him to control this operation.
3. Should the latter request military intervention, your objective will be to assist the civil powers to arrest members of the IRA but subject to the overriding requirement to do all in your power to protect the lives and safety of members of the public and of the security forces.

COMMAND AND CONTROL
4. You will be responsible to the Governor and Commander-in-Chief through his Chief of Staff for the way in which you carry out the military tasks assigned to you. You will act at all times in accordance with the lawful instructions of the senior police officer(s) designated by the Gibraltar Police Commissioner to control this operation.

---

[2] ATO – Ammunition Technical Officer (bomb disposal expert).
[3] Snuffbox – nickname for MI5 operatives.

USE OF FORCE

5. You and your men will not use force unless requested to do so by the Police Commissioner, or unless it is necessary to do so in order to protect life; and you are to comply with rule 6.

6. You and your men may only open fire against a person if you or they have reasonable grounds for believing he/she is currently committing, or is about to commit, an action which is likely to endanger you or their lives or the life of any person, and if there is no other way to prevent this.

FIRING WITHOUT WARNING

7. You and your men may fire without warning if the giving of a warning or any delay in firing could lead to death or injury to you or them or any other person, or if the giving of a warning is clearly impracticable.

WARNING BEFORE FIRING

8. If the circumstances in paragraph 7 do not apply, a warning is necessary before firing. The warning is to include a direction to surrender and a clear warning that fire will be opened if the direction is not obeyed.

AREA OF OPERATIONS

9. Under no circumstances are you or your men to enter Spanish territory or Spanish territorial waters for the purposes connected with Operation Flavius, nor are you or your men to fire at any person on Spanish territory or Spanish territorial waters.

The SAS men were briefed on the basic facts, namely that this was likely to be a PIRA bombing mission carried out by a ruthless and dedicated group of terrorists, but the exact target and the timing was as yet unknown.

For anyone who has not participated in one of the Regiment's briefings, they go something like this. The scene usually resembles a classroom, with rows of chairs set out facing a large-scale Ordnance Survey-type map of the target area resting on a blackboard easel. The team members, notebooks and pens in hand (the wiser ones bringing a Thermos of hot tea as these briefings can go on for hours), then hear an outline of the operation given by the commanding officer, which in a case like this would usually be a major. After the first half-hour or so there may be another speaker, perhaps someone from the 'green slime' (the Intelligence Corps) or a Snuffbox operative, who gives as much information as he or she thinks the soldiers should have on the 'need-to-know' principle. This means that although Intelligence may have a dozen files of information on an individual or a subject, only matters considered by the Intelligence officer will be passed on to the men on the ground. There is of course a good reason for this practice. In the event of too much information being given, the soldier may become confused by what is essentially irrelevant to the mission he is involved in. Also, although this was hardly likely to arise during Operation 'Flavius', prisoners of war cannot give information to the enemy if they do not have it in the first place.

Bordering the commanding officer's displayed map there will usually be, in the case of an anti-terrorist operation, photographs of the likely suspects believed to be involved, and also pictures of any vehicles they are thought to be using with the licence plate numbers. Every SP Team member is taught to write down and memorize the fine detail of a briefing, but when it comes to the actual operation, nothing he has written will be on his person. These notes are purely used as *aides-mémoires* for studying after each updated briefing.

The SP Team chap must be able to recognize his potential target precisely and without the slightest doubt even if beards or other disguises are used, and there is absolutely no room here for mistakes. The briefing officer takes questions from his men at regular periods throughout the meeting and these are usually relaxed and casual enough for the men to voice their doubts and worries. This is not a managing-director-talking-down-to-his-workforce scenario. There's normally a fair amount of banter going on.

In the case of this operation there seemed little that Snuffbox did not know about the bombers and their plan. McCann and Savage had been seen talking outside a bar in the Falls Road on Wednesday, 2 March, and the ASU's commander for the attack was Mairead Farrell. Photographs of the three had already been issued to Spanish police at Málaga airport and it was probable that they would all be travelling on false passports. McCann's would be in the name of either McArdle or Reilly, Savage would be travelling as Coyne, and Farrell, if the intelligence was correct, as Katherine Harper.

Photographs play an exceptionally important role here and if video footage of people or the area is available, so much the better. During the afternoon of Friday, 4 March Mairead Farrell, using a false passport in the name of Katherine Harper, arrived in Málaga on a flight from Brussels. A few hours later, at 8:05 pm, Savage and McCann were spotted by Spanish police as they arrived on Iberian Airways flight IB657 from Paris. They passed through immigration, showing passports in the names of Coyne and Reilly, walked through customs and headed straight for the lavatories in the airport terminal. A few minutes later, as they changed money at a bureau de change, they were joined by Mairead Farrell. Then, unfortunately for Snuffbox, the trio vanished into the night. Although this may sound like a serious flaw in the operation, one needs to understand the practicalities of following suspects without giving the game away.

> When you're tailing someone who's involved in terrorist activities you have to decide how far you're going to expose your people, and the risk of compromising the operation. If they get a glimpse of you at different locations more than once, well that's a compromise. To efficiently tail someone on the move you're talking about a minimum of six people, and if they're mobile [in a car] that then becomes six or more cars with 'hands-off' secure radio communications. These figures are just a rough guide, but to do the job properly you've got to have the resources in manpower. Another important point is that your people must fit in and that means dressed to blend with the surroundings, and old vehicles, not brand new motors out of Hertz Rent-a-Car. In the case of somewhere like Spain there's no point having pale-faced Yorkshiremen trying to look like Latins, it just doesn't work.

Despite Spanish detectives finding the taxi driver who had carried McCann and Savage to the Hotel Florida in Fuengirola, the PIRA team had not booked in there and could not be traced. But then, just after midnight, in a check of hotels in the Málaga area, two Irishmen were reported to have checked into the Hotel Residencia Escandavia in Torremolinos and paid for a three-bedded room for two nights. It was Savage and McCann. But where was Farrell? Snuffbox managed to establish the next morning (Saturday, 5 March) that there were indeed three beds in the room, and that all three had been slept in. Access to the room was by a separate entrance, and anyone entering would not have to pass by the reception desk. It was possible, though not certain, that all three suspects had slept there.

When the occupants went out later that morning Spanish detectives were able to confirm that a woman's makeup was in the room, but did this belong to Farrell? Then word came through that a white Renault 5 had been hired from the nearby Avis car hire office by 'Brendan Coyne' (Savage). While the Renault was being hired by the Irishman named Coyne, Farrell was telephoning the Rent-a-Car Marbesol company in Marbella and asking about terms for hiring a Ford Fiesta.

It should be noted here that up until the actual shootings of the members of the PIRA unit, positive identification of the terrorist trio had not been made. All were travelling on false passports (Farrell flew from Dublin to Brussels using a passport in the name of Johnston), and although all three were suspected of being involved in terrorist activity, neither the Spanish police nor Snuffbox had any concrete evidence to that effect.

Spanish detectives, persuaded by Snuffbox agents that this was an extremely serious affair of international terrorism, discovered that another car-hire company, Autoluis in Torremelinos, had rented a red Ford Escort, registration MA 9317 AF, to an Irishman, John Noakes, who, on Thursday 3 March, had been staying at the A1 Andalus Hotel in Torremolinos. What stuck in the memory of the car-hire clerk was the way that Noakes had begun filling in the rental agreement with one hand (his left) and then switched halfway through to the other. Noakes had been in a great hurry and appeared unnaturally nervous. That weekend it seemed to Snuffbox that there were rather a lot of Irish drivers renting cars on the Costa del Sol, though that, of course, did not mean that one or even any of them were members of PIRA.

Early on Sunday morning McCann and Savage were seen having breakfast together in a bar near the Hotel Residencia Escandavia and then, joined by Farrell, they drove in the Renault 5 to Rent-a-Car Marbesol. The clerk there, Señor Crespo, who had few customers that Sunday, rented Farrell a white Ford Fiesta, registration MA 2732 AJ, which was parked across the street. Farrell paid the deposit in British currency and, thanking the clerk for his help, left the office and climbed into the car. She had some difficulty getting it started and the clerk went outside to help her. When the pair had succeeded in getting the Fiesta going, Farrell asked for directions to Gibraltar, but instead of going the way Crespo had indicated she drove away from the car-hire office and straight into the basement of the nearby Edificio Marbeland car park.

That Sunday, seven male and female Snuffbox agents, each carrying a secure radio with a miniature voice-activated microphone and an earphone, were on watch in Gibraltar. Their controller, 'M,'[4] and the SAS major were studying a large-scale street map of the city in the specially prepared Operation 'Flavius' control room. The SP Team's operational commander, an SAS captain, waited for an updated sitrep with the unit's ATO (bomb disposal expert), codenamed 'Felix', and four other SAS men. Dressed in jeans and casual jackets each of the SP Troop men carried a 9mm Browning Hi-Power pistol and four magazines. Their guns were not in holsters, but tucked into the waistbands of their trousers and covered by their jackets.

'M' was worried. If the PIRA unit turned up in Gibraltar that day the first news of their arrival would come from the Gibraltar frontier post where a local Special Branch officer, Detective Constable Charles

---

[4] 'M' was the codename used by this MI5 officer at the inquest.

Huart, was sitting in an enclosed Spanish Immigration office watching, on a screen, passports being checked.

In their attempts to keep a low-profile in order not to be noticed by the PIRA unit it now looked as if the Spanish police had lost them altogether.

The First Sighting

And then suddenly, one of the Snuffbox agents spots Sean Savage. The time is 2:30 pm and Savage is there in Gibraltar's main square. He is wearing a pinstriped jacket and blue jeans. Turning away, the agent whispers into his concealed microphone that he thinks, no, he is sure, that Savage is in the square. Over the radio net the major and 'M' hear a signal from another pair of agents confirming the sighting of Farrell and McCann, who appear to have just crossed the border on foot. Now Savage is wandering back across the square and is unlocking the driver's door of a white Renault 5, parked with its bonnet against a wall. This is the square where the Royal Anglian Regiment band is due to play. A quick check by telephone with Spanish police confirms that the licence plate on the Renault matches a hire car rented in Spain.

Savage opens the door and is then seen to be doing something inside, but the watcher cannot see exactly what he is up to without appearing too interested. As Savage loiters near the Renault, Mairead Farrell and Daniel McCann are still walking towards the town centre. The ATO with the team is immediately sent out from the operations room to have a discreet look at the car. To him there is no obvious sign that the vehicle might contain a bomb. The car seems normal, not out of balance the way it might be if it were carrying a heavy bomb. And then he notices the aerial. It is a relatively new car but the aerial looks old and rusty, suggesting to him that it might have been added later for one purpose: to receive the command signal for a radio-detonated bomb. At 2:50 pm Farrell and McCann join Savage near the car and then the three begin a leisurely stroll together through the town, all the while being watched by the Snuffbox team.

> It was pretty clear that what they were doing was one of the oldest tricks in the undercover book, testing the air to see if they could spot a surveillance team. Whether the Renault had a bomb in it or not was unknown at this stage and the only way to find out was pull it apart. That would have meant clearing the public out of the area and probably watching the bombers leg it gently back across the border. The ATO experts had been picking up an odd transmission signal coming from over the Spanish border for some time that they couldn't identify, and this made them think that there was a chance the PIRA gang might be working on a long-distance detonation. Recent experiences in Northern Ireland had shown that PIRA had some pretty sophisticated gear for detonating car bombs from great distances.

The Contact

At 3:40 pm, on receiving news of the PIRA teams' activities, the Police Commissioner Joseph Canepa gives his authorization by telephone for the SAS to take over responsibility for the operation. Now the three suspects are walking back through the town towards the Spanish border. Suddenly Savage separates from the others and turns to walk back in the direction of the Renault. The four SP Team soldiers who are now observing them from both sides of the street try not to be noticed. There are people on the street but not enough to vanish among. Everyone is exposed to observant eyes. As he walks back towards them, Savage bumps shoulders with one of the SAS men, codename ALPHA, but carries on walking. The SAS men separate. CHARLIE and DELTA with a woman Snuffbox agent, JULIET, follow Savage, while ALPHA and BRAVO stay behind Farrell and McCann.

Just before 4 pm a police inspector who is unaware of the operation (under the 'need-to-know' rule only those directly involved in 'Flavius' had knowledge of it) receives a radio message in his marked police car to return to base immediately, and he turns on his siren to cut through heavy traffic in the town. In fact he is being recalled so that his car can be available to collect three PIRA prisoners Gibraltar police expect to arrest that afternoon. On hearing the siren, Farrell and McCann become noticeably jumpy and start looking around them.

Then suddenly the game is up, for McCann makes eye contact with one of the SAS men. From a distance of about ten metres their eyes lock. In a split second, ALPHA goes for his gun. He is about to issue a shouted warning when McCann, who is looking at him over his left shoulder, makes a sudden movement with his right arm which disappears from ALPHA's view. Where is that right hand going, for a gun or to trigger a bomb? The risk is too great. In one smooth and practised movement ALPHA cradles the Browning with both hands, extends his arms towards the target and fires one round into McCann's back. At the same moment Mairead Farrell makes a sudden gesture towards her handbag and ALPHA shoots her too with a single round. In the seconds that follow both soldiers fire rapidly at the two PIRA volunteers, while in a lane that leads to Landport tunnel a short distance away, Savage spins round on hearing the shots. One of the two soldiers following him, CHARLIE, shouts 'STOP!' but as he does so, Savage's right hand moves suddenly towards his pocket. Both SAS men CHARLIE and DELTA open fire. The time is 4:06 pm. Moments later McCann, Farrell and Savage are dead.

The SAS men, still covering their lifeless victims in case one of them moves, move forward to search the bodies for firearms or explosive devices. A few moments later, however, they discover that none of the three PIRA members is armed. 'Felix', the bomb expert, is examining the white Renault 5 in the square which is being cleared of members of the public. He can't believe it. Snuffbox has got it wrong. The car is clean.

Postscript

What happened in the last moments of the lives of Savage, McCann and Farrell has become a *cause célèbre* for those who accuse the SAS of being the British government's 'Special Assassination Squad'. Why, they ask were the three suspects not arrested or, failing that, shot in the arm or the leg? The question, to any trooper who has served on an anti-terrorist operation, is ludicrous. All the evidence available to the SP Team suggested that this was to be an impressive bombing operation by three ruthless, determined and experienced terrorists and that evidence, gathered over a period of four months by RUC Special Branch and MI5 had left little doubt in their minds that a split second might mean the difference between life and death.

At the inquest held in Gibraltar, the first soldier to open fire recalled: 'McCann looked over his left shoulder. He was smiling. He looked straight at me. The smile went off his face. It is hard to describe but it was as though he knew who I was or that I was a threat to him.' Then McCann made a sudden movement across his body. 'I thought he was definitely going to go for a button.' He fired one round at McCann. 'I saw Farrell grabbing at her handbag. I thought she was going for the button so I shot her once in the back.' SAS soldiers are taught to shoot their target until that target ceases to be a threat. When the shooting stopped, McCann had two bullet wounds in his body, three to the head. Farrell died from an internal haemorrhage when three bullets entered her back, passed through her chest and exited in the front. She also had two bullet wounds to the head. Professor Alan Watson, the Crown pathologist suggested at the inquest that she was shot in the head first and was facing her attacker at the time. The three torso wounds were probably fired, he added, from a distance of between two and six feet.

Sean Savage, who was the last to die, was hit by a total of 'sixteen to eighteen bullets'. The coroner was unsure exactly how many rounds had hit him, adding that 'there were, in all, twenty-seven wounds to his body'.

The two key points in the matter, as far as the SAS men and British law are concerned, lie in the rules of engagement orders issued to the CRW team, rules which also apply in the Northern Ireland conflict. The SAS unit says the British government had reasonable belief that the PIRA unit planned to detonate a bomb, and that they used reasonable force to stop the terrorists. Whatever the opinion of the reader, being asked to stop a potentially armed bomber from killing and maiming innocent civilians, and without getting oneself killed in the process, is a task which most people would be unwilling to try and incapable of carrying out.

Giving evidence at the inquest, one of the soldiers who shot Savage said:

In our rules of engagement if we thought the threat was so great we had no need to give a warning. We knew the fact the bomb was there. We knew Savage could well be carrying the device to detonate the bomb. With him making such violent movements, we didn't even need to give him a warning.

Facing its critics, the SAS is adamant that the SP Team did the right thing in the circumstances. One ex-special forces soldier said:

In anyone's book tracking three dangerous terrorists across Europe and foiling their plan without loss of civilian or military life is a rare thing. The only draw-back is that at the time of the ambush the three were not actually committing an offence. It was just the recce. But quite honestly we didn't know that. For us that is not an issue; not much sleep was lost over that. Guys put their lives on the line and some elements in our society would rather support killers like the IRA. That is upsetting.

After the shootings, Spanish authorities were told by Gibraltar police that a red Ford Fiesta car MA 9317 AF parked in La Linea, across the border from Gibraltar, might contain a bomb. When they checked no bomb was found, but they did discover in the glove compart-ment a keyring marked with a large letter E and a set of keys for another Fiesta. When Spanish police searched the car park of the Hotel Residencia Escandavia in Tor-remolinos they found a white Fiesta MA 2732 AJ with 64 kilos of Semtex in the boot.

The bombers' plan, as detectives pieced it together later, was to drive Farrell's white Fiesta into Gibraltar three days later and park it in the space occupied by the Renault. A simple timer, and not a sophisticated remote-control device, was to have been used to explode the bomb.

At the inquest into the deaths, a senior British Intelligence officer admitted that three wrong assumptions had been made: they believed the trio to be armed; they thought the Renault contained a bomb; and they believed that the explosion would be initiated by a remote-control device.

On hearing of the ruling by the European Court of Human Rights that 'the British Government had used more force than was absolutely necessary in Gibraltar', Deputy Prime Minister Michael Heseltine declared that their decision 'was incomprehensible and defied common sense'.

The man calling himself John Noakes, who had hired the red Fiesta MA 9317 AF, has never been found.

NINE

OPERATION GRANBY – THE GULF

For many in the Regiment who were deployed during the Gulf conflict, it seemed like history repeating itself. A number of them had already operated in the deserts of the Arabian peninsula, though the SAS in general was more at home in the rugged terrain of Oman. For most, however, it was time to learn, as David Stirling and Jock Lewes had been obliged to do in the Second World War – and some of them had to learn fast.

Since their days operating against the Adoo in Oman and the heroic battle at Mirbat, the Regiment had trained regularly in desert warfare in friendly Gulf states. The SAS maintains its links with the Sultan of Oman's Special Forces, among others, and has been responsible for training many of that region's elite units and close-protection teams. Towards the end of 1990, in the wake of Iraq's invasion of Kuwait, A, B, and D Squadrons were deployed to the Gulf, effectively leaving G Squadron and the Northern Ireland Troop to look after just about all other SAS business.

In charge of British special forces desert operations was a seasoned military commander, Brigadier Andrew

Massey. After much lobbying by General Sir Peter de la Billière who knew the area of operations well having served with the Regiment in Oman in the 1970s, US General Norman Schwarzkopf, Commander-in-Chief of the Allied multinational force, gave his agreement for SAS operations to begin. For some who took part in behind-the-lines operations in that short but bloody war in 1991, this was the task they had been waiting for. Now they had the opportunity of fighting an enemy on their own terms, with the gloves off, and in exactly the way that the Regiment's founder had envisaged for them.

In the forty-three days during which they operated inside Iraq, SAS and SBS troops dealt their enemy many hard blows, but most importantly, they located and destroyed Iraq's Scud missile force. From the first day of planning, Massey was told that the SAS's role would be exclusively to render the Scud threat harmless, and that it did not matter what methods his teams employed to accomplish that task. He had three battle-hardened squadrons of Britain's finest troops, and in theory just about all the weaponry he could ask for. A and D Squadron were deployed in desert vehicles, usually specially equipped Landrovers still known to the men as 'Pink Panthers', from the colour of their desert camouflage. By the end of January there were four mobile SAS columns operating behind enemy lines, and on 12 February, so confident were the patrol leaders, a convoy of ten four-ton trucks crossed over from Saudi Arabia to re-equip them at Wadi Tubal.

Some of the encounters between SAS patrols and the enemy were extremely fierce, lasting in one case almost four and a half hours, but most of the operations involved locating and attacking Scud operating sites and pinpointing them for Allied aircraft attacks. By 4 March, the last SAS patrol had left enemy territory, their job done. Casualties had been very slight considering the dangers of operating behind enemy lines and in such hostile terrain.

Less fortunate were some of the B Squadron men who, on arriving at the SAS's forward operating base of Al Jawf in Saudi Arabia, found that the best vehicles and a lot of the specialized equipment they would need had already been procured by A and D Squadrons. One or two ex-members of the Regiment have suggested that the enthusiasm shown by a few SAS men to 'get over the border' led to unnecessary risks being taken; however, to have missed the opportunity for action in the Gulf would for most of them have been unthinkable, in spite of the risk to their lives. At the time, fifty years after David Stirling had taken on Rommel in the Western Desert, the SAS was once again going to fight in a real desert war, just as their founder had done. Many would discover the grim reality of warfare in such a deadly environment.

One of the best documented accounts of an SAS operation which, it has to be said, went horribly wrong is that by Sergeant Andy McNab (not his real name), who arrived in Saudi Arabia with B Squadron and deployed to the forward operating base at Al Jawf. Normally used to working in the standard four-man patrols, McNab and another sergeant, Vince Phillips, were called to a meeting with B Squadron's commanding officer, who explained that he had a task for them and issued a warning order. That order lays out in rough parameters what the job is going to be, and it also lets the men know that until the planning stage is complete, there will be no other movement of the team, which in this case would be an eight-man patrol.

Since they would be so isolated behind the enemy lines, enlarging the force from the traditional four-man unit to eight seemed to make sense, as this would give increased firepower and enable them to cause more havoc. When McNab discovered that the limited supply of prized Pink Panthers had already been signed out to teams from other squadrons, his heart sank. There were other Landrovers available, the 110s, but unlike the Panthers, these were not specifically designed or specially equipped for overland desert operations. After much head scratching he decided on the other option; Bravo Two-Zero, his patrol's radio call sign, would go in on foot with a night insertion by Chinook helicopter.

Whether that decision was the correct one to take at the time is open to conjecture, but often when faced with life-and-death decisions, as one veteran says, 'You can sometimes think too long about the rights and wrongs. In the end you just go for it.' The men of McNab's patrol began to prepare for their task, which was primarily to find and cut the enemy's communication links between Baghdad and the Scud teams who were operating in north-west Iraq. If these links were severed, the Scud operators would not know where or when to attack. What was required from the patrol was the maximum effect with the minimum of effort, and the first job was to find the telecommunications land line that ran along the northern main supply route (MSR) from Baghdad to Jordan. The second task was simply to attack the Scuds wherever and whenever they were found. There were a number of ways they could do that. They could call in an air attack, keeping the Scud launchers under observation and talking the aircraft in on to their targets by radio; they could make a stand-off attack, which involved hitting the sites with LAW-66 anti-tank rockets; or, if neither of those options were feasible, they would make a hands-on attack, which meant prime-target assassinations of the surveyors and operators, and the demolition of the transporter erector/launchers, rather than the Scuds themselves.

There was a good reason for attacking the launchers rather than the Scuds. The worrying aspect of the planned operation was that it was believed at the time that some of the Scuds carried binary warheads (a binary weapon is a projectile divided into two components, each containing a different substance; on detonation, these combine to produce a nerve gas), and McNab and his team certainly did not want to be around when one of those exploded. Searching the quartermaster's stores at Al Jawf for the equipment they needed, McNab and his men were dismayed to find that it was not only the Pink Panthers that had gone. Most of the kit they needed, like anti-personnel mines and rounds for their M203s, had also been snapped up by men from the other squadrons. There were no suppressed (reduced-noise) weapons available for knocking out enemy sentries, and when Chris Ryan, one of the patrol, asked about Claymore mines, he was told to find himself some plastic explosive and improvise with empty ice-cream cartons.

McNab's men were far from being on the point of mutiny, but one or two were clearly not happy with the shortages of specialized kit, and there were some nagging doubts as to whether the team was fully prepared for the task ahead. To say that such doubts are extraordinary or unusual when men are about to go into battle and risk their lives while surrounded on all sides by their enemies would be misleading, as every SAS veteran has experienced such feelings on the eve of a mission. The realization that tomorrow may be your last day on earth is something that professional soldiers have to learn to live with, especially those who wear the SAS beret. McNab told his men that they would just have to make do with what was available, and that in the end they would manage. After all, they were the SAS, and improvisation is what the Regiment is good at. When the eight men had packed their heavily laden bergens and filled their belt-kits with water bottles and ammunition, they had difficulty in standing up. To do so they had to put their bergens on sitting down and then pull one another on to their feet. Each soldier was carrying around 90 kilos of weapons, ammunition, explosives and other assorted kit, more than most of them weighed! How on earth were they going to operate carrying such huge loads? It was decided that they would make a cache area in the desert where they could store water and other less essential items, and having carefully concealed their reserves they would then operate in the normal way, returning to resupply themselves when necessary.

On the night of 22 January, the eight-man Bravo Two-Zero patrol flew into Iraq. Shortly after crossing the Saudi Arabian border their Chinook helicopter was suddenly illuminated by what they believe was the radar of a Roland ground-to-air missile. It was heading straight for them, and usually they don't miss. McNab recalls that at this point the helicopter crew 'really had to earn their money', taking drastic evasive action which is pretty difficult when you are travelling at 80 knots and flying only 20 or so metres above the ground. Having succeeded in avoiding the Roland, the helicopter eventually reached Bravo Two-Zero's drop-off point, which was to the south of the MSR.

While four team members took up positions away from the helicopter to get out of the dust kicked up by its rotor blades and to give themselves clear arcs of fire, the others rushed to unload bergens, plastic jerry cans of water, and munitions that they would soon need in order to survive. One jerry can would be used to urinate in, just in case wild animals became attracted by the scent of hidden OPs and drew attention to the patrol's presence. For other bodily functions the men would have to squat over a plastic sheet, stowing the human waste care-fully back into their bergens, just as they had done in Northern Ireland.

As the helicopter lifted off, McNab and his men saw their first Scud launch, west of them and about ten kilometres away. He recalls, 'We couldn't do anything about it at that stage. The cache area was about twenty kilometres away and that was going to be our operating base.' The group arrived there while it was still dark, and the next morning, lying flat in the open on high ground they tried to send their first sitrep. They had no response to their transmissions, and so immediately went into what is known as 'lost comms' procedure. The men were not especially concerned as this sort of thing happens occasionally, but one or two of them were starting to worry. Premonitions are taken very seriously in the SAS, and things were not looking too rosy. At about 4:30 pm, after lying up all day, they heard goats, which inevitably meant that there were people around to look after the animals, but for McNab this was 'no big problem because we were in good cover and no tracks led to our LUP [lying-up position]'.

What were going to be problems, however, as they would shortly find out, were the Iraqi twin S-60 anti-aircraft guns parked 200 metres from Bravo Two-Zero's hideout – and a young boy, a goatherd aged about five or six, who suddenly walked towards their position. The game was up. 'His eyes went as big as saucers, he knew what was going on and went screaming off to the [Iraqi anti-aircraft] guns.' The patrol had been compromised, but there was no time for panic; they had a job to do and well-practised routines to follow.

The first priority was to get as much water and carbohydrate 'down their necks', for in the hours that would follow they knew there would be no time for eating. Having filled all their water bottles to the brim again, the men began to move out, wrapping their shemaghs around their faces in the hope that any enemy soldiers looking at them with binoculars might think they were an Iraqi foot patrol. The fact that Iraqi soldiers rarely walked anywhere and spent most of their time being carried in the backs of trucks was not important. There was just a chance, even if it was a slim one, that they might get away without trouble. But it was not to be.

A bulldozer appeared, trying to get up on to the MSR which McNab's team had come all this way to observe, and then, after the patrol had walked quickly for about 500 metres, they came under fire from the east. Two Iraqi armoured cars with turret-mounted 7.62mm machine guns were bearing down on them, backed up by another armoured vehicle carrying infantry. They decided to stand and fight and went into action, first dropping their bergens and then moving forward. 'The contact was initiated by us, purely because it's going to happen and there's nothing you can do so you just get on with it and get it over and done.' The area in which they found themselves fighting for their lives was flat plain with very little cover. In the minutes that followed a vicious firefight raged, but amazingly none of the SAS men were hit.

At one point they managed to retrieve their bergens and began a hair-raising withdrawal from the battlefield, but then the S-60 anti-aircraft guns opened up and things started looking serious again. It was now starting to get dark, and after forty minutes of combat, the night was closing in to cover them. McNab recalls, 'It was the darkness that got us away. It was then I made

the decision that we would have to escape and evade.'
Syria was 178 kilometres away from their present position, and that, they decided, was both the nearest and the best safe place to head for. Iraqi troops would undoubtedly expect them to go the other way, back towards the Saudi Arabian border.

There were far more enemy troops in Bravo Two-Zero's area of operation than intelligence reports had predicted – in excess of 3,000 Iraqis, as it turned out. It seemed clear to McNab that he and his men had stumbled on the worst possible place in the whole of Iraq in which to set up an OP, with the possible exception of the centre of Baghdad. What made matters worse was that they were not sure if their sitrep radio messages had been received, and the section transceiver had been abandoned by its operator during the firefight. All they had now were their TACBE sets, which are radio 'tactical distress beacons' designed for sending 'Maydays' and for calling in rescue helicopters. These work on an international distress frequency and the men had been told that there was a twenty-four-hour watch on them. All you had to do was pull the pin and speak. Within fifteen seconds, they had been promised, a very calm, usually female, operator will respond, trying to reassure you that help and rescue is on the way while you are screaming into the mouthpiece pleading for an air strike and a casevac (casualty evacuation). But the TACBEs didn't work. McNab and his men called and called. There was nothing. The AWACS aircraft which should have responded to their 'Turbo' calls were flying around Saudi Arabia more than 300 kilometres to the south, and aboard the aircraft nothing was heard.

During their night getaway and in driving rain while still being pursued by Iraqi troops, Bravo Two-Zero put in a deception plan by heading south for 20 kilometres, then dog-legging west for 10 before turning north to cross the MSR again. While stopping to hold a 'Chinese Parliament' (a quick discussion about the situation) after another brief firefight, three of the patrol ahead of McNab were lost in the darkness and the rain, and despite desperate attempts to find them using their TACBEs and PNV goggles, they were nowhere to be seen.

Worst of all, one man was going down with hypothermia, and it was then that McNab decided to try and hijack a vehicle. This, he decided, was the only way he and his remaining men were going to get out of Iraq alive. Reaching the MSR again, McNab set up an OP and waited. Before long he saw Toyota Land Cruisers, trucks and other vehicles using the road, and he and Bob Consiglio left their weapons and belt-kit with the other three and waved down the next vehicle that approached them from the west. This turned out to be a yellow 1950s New York cab. They commandeered the vehicle and headed off, with McNab driving and Steve Lane navigating, using his compass and an almost useless small-scale aeronautical chart with which the men had been issued.

Soon they were travelling through built-up areas that bore no relation to the map, and finally, while heading west, they ran into a checkpoint about eleven kilometres from the Syrian border. They were boxed in by vehicles jammed together on the busy road. They knew there was no way they were going to be able to talk their way through, so McNab initiated a firefight which basically involved 'a lot of firepower and all [of us] getting out and running away quickly'. The men knew that the contact area would be swarming with enemy troops that night and the next day, so their only option was to try to get out as quickly as possible under the cover of darkness.

They kept heading west and were now close to the banks of the Euphrates River and the Syrian border.

Once again they were spotted, and another firefight ensued. 'We'd come up against some anti-aircraft guns which their infantry started firing so the only way was to head north and go through a built-up area.' It was here, on the banks of the river, that McNab and his four comrades would fight and some would die – only 10 kilometres away from the safety of the Syrian frontier. There was chaos, the nightmare of the running, fighting soldier facing overwhelming odds, who knows deep down in his guts that his chances of escape and ultimate survival are running out. It was now eleven o'clock at night, and the running battle lasted into the early hours of the morning. By then, Bravo Two-Zero was formally missing in action.

The details of McNab's capture, subsequent interrogation and torture at the hands of his Iraqi captors were graphically illustrated in his book, *Bravo Two-Zero*, which raced to the top of the best-seller lists. Chris Ryan, who had joined 22 SAS from the Territorial Army (he had been in 23 SAS) and was the only member of the patrol to reach Syria and friendly territory, painted a similar dramatic picture of that fateful operation in his own book, though some of the detail varies. One might call this inevitable, as two observers rarely tell the same story about an event, but it is clear that from the start of the planning phase there was friction between the two men, and the decision to operate on foot in such hostile conditions, most especially in the worst weather that had been experienced in that region for many years, suggests a certain lack of foresight.

One hardened veteran who fought in Oman in the 1970s with A Squadron said, 'It was crazy going in on foot with all that kit. Most of them couldn't even stand up properly with their bergens on.' In fact, the other two B Squadron foot patrols, One-Zero and Three-Zero, opted for extraction instead of remaining at their drop-off points. The first patrol pulled out immediately when the officer leading them saw the ground, while the other remained for an hour before asking for a helicopter to pull them out. In retrospect it is easy to criticize the planning and leadership of Bravo Two-Zero's mission, and some experts have suggested that the 'gung-ho' factor played a part in their decision to operate inside Iraq on foot. It is clear that for many serving SAS soldiers the Gulf War was an opportunity too good to miss, for such conflicts occur quite rarely.

Some of the patrol's members had never participated in what they would have called a 'real war', and this was a chance for them to perform with skill and perhaps heroism. All of Bravo Two-Zero's members had practical battle experience, and all showed tremendous courage, but as any experienced veteran will tell you, when things go wrong in warfare, they usually go very, very wrong. Despite the disasters that hit McNab's patrol, however, the men fought with great bravery against overwhelming odds in terrain that one SAS soldier described as 'a billiard table'.

A veteran of D Squadron operations who saw action many times in Oman, Northern Ireland and half-a-dozen less-publicized wars, recalled escape and evasion exercises during the 1970s:

It's like they tell you in training, move at night, lie up in the day. The secret is good navigation and attention to detail. Whenever someone tried to be a bit clever, tried cutting corners, they usually came unstuck. We did E&E exercises across France where you'd move cross-country at night. As long as you stuck to the rules which have been developed carefully over the years, you stood a good chance of getting through. Personally, I never got caught once.

The SAS teams that operated with vehicles far behind the Iraqi lines had, like the men of Bravo Two-Zero, to face the elements as well as the enemy, and quickly adapted themselves to the harsh weather conditions just as their Second World War predecessors had done. Over their flimsy desert combat fatigues they wore locally made Arab coats, sometimes with Arctic-style duvet jackets underneath, and fleece-lined cold-weather hats which are more frequently seen on NATO operations in Norway. Added to this cold-weather kit most of the men sported the Bedouin-style shemagh, just as the SAS Originals had done in the Western Desert fifty years earlier.

As well as specially adapted long-wheelbase Land-rovers, the Regiment deployed a small fleet of fast trail motorcycles which acted as forward scouts for the heavily armoured patrols, their lightly armed riders carrying out valuable work, before returning to a 'mother ship' for refuelling. Moving mostly at night and lying up during the day under huge camouflage nets that hid their vehicles, many valuable lessons were learnt, while, amazingly, casualties were slight. On one occasion, SAS soldiers held a full sergeants' mess meeting miles behind the enemy lines while lookouts kept an attentive eye on the horizon in case an enemy patrol should show. The main subject of debate was whether they should invest in some rather expensive chairs for the refurbished mess in Hereford. When the meeting concluded, the men returned to their less mundane duties and went back to the war.

Using state-of-the-art navigation equipment, which included hand-held Magellan ground-positioning systems, SAS teams guided Allied planes on to enemy Scud launching sites and other targets of opportunity. In one of many successful night actions, a patrol from D Squadron, numbering eight vehicles, guided American bombers on to a Scud launching site deep inside Iraq. The main concern of the patrol's commander was the risk of a 'blue-on-blue', the danger of being bombed by friendly forces. A cost-saving decision by the Ministry of Defence not to fit 'identification-friend-or-foe' (IFF) systems to British vehicles would lead to one horrendous accident during the war in which an American A-10 aircraft attacked a British armoured patrol, causing several tragic deaths.

The radio conversation between the SAS patrol, call sign Delta Two-One, showed their concern:

> *SAS radio operator:* Aircraft, this is Delta Two-One . . . our location three-three one-two zero-three north, zero-four two-two east.
> *US pilot:* Stand by, we're looking . . . take a mark point . . . I got it, I got it . . . bombs away, bombs away! Smack!
> *SAS radio operator:* Attack aircraft, this is Highlight . . . that was on target, on target. Be aware there are my friendly forces, eight vehicles total in the open five hundred metres north and west. Your original target was three [Scud] launchers plus associated vehicles by the burning light.
> *US pilot:* Bombs away! Bombs away! Street seven you've got 'em now, we're going home.

Details of other covert operations carried out by British special forces during the war are less precise, and include stories that a team of SAS men had boarded the last British Airways flight to Kuwait just as Iraqi troops were crossing the border in their invasion of the country. The Ministry of Defence, true to its policy of never discussing special forces operations, would neither confirm nor deny suggestions in the *Independent* that a scheduled flight had been used for covert insertion of an SAS team, but then, as one retired NCO with a droopy desperado moustache quipped with a grin, 'You wouldn't expect them to admit to that, would you?' Whether this did or did not happen will no doubt be revealed in later tales from Hereford, but the writer can only confirm that the SAS has the nerve and guile required to carry out such a mission.

What is certain is that the Headshed in Hereford was very much aware of the losing battle being fought by a handful of courageous resistance fighters in Kuwait City, who carried out some heroic and very risky hit-and-run raids on Iraqi forces there. In spite of the presence of Iraq's elite Republican Guard who searched foreign residences and painted white crosses on doors to show they had been searched, expatriates hiding in the city managed to stay in touch with each other, and to communicate with the outside world using fax machines and messengers. Sometimes hiding in cupboards during the day and only coming out at night, they even managed to produce a newsletter, complete with cartoons showing Saddam Hussein in a variety of embarrassing situations. An attempt by British and other expatriates to make a run for the Saudi border was discouraged by Foreign Office planners and their military advisers, in order to avoid needless loss of life.

One early plan to insert members of B Squadron into Kuwait City so that they could set up an OP in a high-rise building was shelved as soon as the Scud threat appeared. Brigadier Andy Massey's brief was simple and direct: 'Scud, Scud, and nothing but Scud'. It was plainly clear to Massey that the greatest risk to the Coalition was that of Israel being dragged into the war. There was a strong possibility that if this happened the delicate alliance between Arab and Western forces might break, so that everything that could be done to prevent this was held to be of vital importance.

Compared with other campaigns in which the Regiment has fought, SAS losses were relatively light, especially considering the dangers. McNab's Bravo Two-Zero patrol lost three men killed, Sergeant Vince Phillips, Corporal Steven Lane and Trooper Bob Consiglio – the last two were each awarded the Military Medal. The other SAS man killed behind enemy lines was Lance-Corporal David 'Shug' Denbury, QGM, MM, a motorcycle scout who, as has been said earlier, was shot in a running battle with Iraqi troops. McNab and his three fellow prisoners of war were released after the ceasefire and like Chris Ryan, the only member of Bravo Two-Zero to reach freedom in Syria, received warm welcomes and decorations on their return. A member of R Squadron commented, 'The medals always go to the wrong people . . .' That remark, like many made by SAS soldiers, is common in Regiment circles, for often the work carried out by men in the field is unseen and subsequently unrewarded.

TEN

BLACK OPS, GREEN OPS

The battles that the Regiment is fighting today and
those it will fight into the next century are likely to be
even more clandestine affairs than those that have gone
before. Since the formation of the SAS's Counter-Revolutionary Warfare (CRW) Wing[1] in the aftermath of the
1972 Munich Olympics when German border guards
bungled an attempt to rescue Israeli hostages, the Regiment's precise role has increasingly widened. While sat-
isfying the nation's requirement for a covert but
uniformed military force, elements of the SAS have for
several years been trained for what they themselves
refer to as 'Black Operations'.

Unlike Green Operations, which are those for which
standard disruptive pattern material (DPM) or predominantly green military clothing are worn – in the
United Kingdom or abroad – Black Ops normally
involve the wearing of 'siege-busting' kit: blue-black
fire-retardant coveralls, gas masks and body armour,
which were first seen by the public at the Iranian
Embassy siege in 1980 (see Chapter Five). This demar-
cation between the types of mission is not, as some
might suggest, a key to other more covert operations in

---

[1] As has been said, the Counter-Revolutionary Warfare Wing is
known inside the SAS today as the Special Projects Team (SP Team).

which the Regiment's members take part. Today's 22 Special Air Service is not trained solely to combat military and terrorist threats. It is also available – and is specially equipped – to counter civil unrest and armed insurrection at home or abroad.

In October 1987, SAS men stormed Scotland's Peterhead prison using CS gas, stun grenades and riot batons to free an injured prison officer who was being held hostage. The Regiment's involvement was not made public, and although there was press speculation at the time that the SAS had been involved in the rescue, details of this Black Op. were kept quiet.

While most of the operations in which the Regiment participates today remain secret, a glance at recent history shows more than ever, that it is still in the front line of covert military and security force missions. The decision to deploy an SAS reconnaissance team can be made in a few hours.

Let's imagine we've got something going on in a friendly country and through the Foreign Office, COBRA (Cabinet Office Briefing Room) and the JOC (Joint Operations Centre) comes a request for help. The President [of the friendly country] gets word that his uncle has seized power, and Mr President, wife, kids and his loyal bodyguard are holed up in the palace, bullets coming in through the curtains, they're surrounded by nasties. Or perhaps it's a British Airways jumbo full of Brits that's been seized at the airport by the revolutionary-minded uncle or some obscure terrorist group that nobody's ever heard of.

In the majority of capital cities you've got either an embassy or a consulate whose knowledge of local history and politics is excellent, and often the defence attaché will pass on a pretty accurate sitrep which the Headshed will be able to interpret. Those guys, unlike the Consul or the Ambassador, normally speak our language and know the difference between a Scud and a Katyusha 'Stalin Organ' [a Soviet-built multi-barrelled rocket launcher]. Straightaway 'the Kremlin' (Planning and Intelligence) gets going amassing the info, working out who's who and what's going on. When the Gulf War was in progress, Bush and his defence advisers got updated reports from CNN every hour. Even though some of the facts you see on TV turn out later to be wrong, video tape showing what a particular group is wearing, what kind of weapons they're using can be invaluable to a guy that's about to find himself inserted.

In the first instance, no matter where in the world it may be, a reconnaissance of the target is needed. While satellite photographs (ELINT) today can read the number plate of a car and, under ideal climatic conditions, can even identify the rank of an officer and differentiate between foreign armies' units, the presence of eyes on the ground (HUMINT) is the most important asset special forces operations can have.

An example of this occurred in the Gambia in July 1981. While the President, Sir Dawda Jawara, was attending the marriage ceremony of Prince Charles and Lady Diana in St Paul's Cathedral, a well-timed locally inspired coup, backed up by Cuban and Libyan agents threw the capital, Banjul, into chaos. The commanding officer of the SAS who was hillwalking in the Brecon Beacons, was informed and he immediately contacted his second-in-command, Major Ian Crooke. On 29 July Crooke was given an outline of the situation with instructions to get to the Gambia as quickly as possible, liaise with the President who was already on his way home from London, and give as much assistance and advice as he could. Not only had President Jawara been overthrown, the rebels were holding members of his family, and as well as taking over the capital they had captured Bakau, a small town on the coast. The British High Commission had been cut off and scores of British nationals were missing. Greatly liked and respected by the soldiers who had served with him in Oman (troopers and NCOs often referred to him as 'Crookie', though they used the more usual 'Boss' to his face), Crooke had no difficulty finding two experienced NCOs for the mission.

Never one to waste time or get bogged down in the complicated and often dull aspects of administration, the major packed the equipment he considered important for the operation in zipper holdalls and made some secure-communications phone calls. He discovered that friendly Senegalese forces had moved against the rebels; they had already recaptured Banjul, and a scheduled Air France flight to neighbouring Dacca on 2 August would bring him and his team close to the action. A personal friend of Crooke was in charge of Air France security, and the airline agreed discreetly to carry his arsenal of Heckler & Kochs, Browning pistols, stun grenades, two-way radios and the rest of a highly explosive cargo which would normally be banned on civilian flights.

Major Crooke and his two sergeants flew to Dacca via Paris, and after reassuring the extremely worried President Jawara that matters would be resolved as quickly as possible, and that the rescue of his wife, brother and six children were the SAS men's first priority, he linked up with friendly Senegalese forces and began his planning. It looked bad. Estimates of between 400 and 500 well-equipped rebels scattered in and around seafront buildings on the Atlantic coast, where they were holding a similar number of British and European citizens hostage, did little to encourage the

SAS men. Crooke decided the best thing he could do was to go and have a look.

Although the latest satellite communications equipment had come into service around that time, enabling the team to stay in constant touch with the Headshed, sometimes there are occasions when the man in the field would rather not be disturbed.

> Certainly good comms are vital to an operation like the Gambia. But when all's said and done, the last thing you want when you're only three men and you're recceing behind the enemy lines is the Colonel coming on the phone and asking what's going on, have you done this, have you done that. They might not have liked being in the dark for a while but Crookie knew what he was doing. Just look at the result.

Crooke discovered a weak point in the enemy's defences by carrying out some cunning night manoeuvres along the coast road. He knew that the rebels were in control of the area around the British High Commission and that the President's family were prisoners in the health centre near by. Returning to the Gambian and Senegalese army lines, he explained his rapidly conceived rescue plan to their commanders. Meanwhile, his two NCOs began holding a late-night course in tactics in the rather misguided hope that the indigenous forces could be trained very quickly in SAS-style operations. Someone suggested to Crooke that it might be better to hang fire and wait for reinforcements to be sent out from Hereford, but this he decided would waste valuable time. What if the rebels began executing their prisoners?

Next day the carefully planned advance on the enemy stronghold began. It was a fiasco. Crooke therefore decided to take matters in his own hands and, armed to the teeth and dressed in civilian shirts and slacks, the SAS men drove straight through the enemy's lines and parked outside the medical centre. The two guards at the front of the building were astonished to see this cheerful and apparently unarmed white man marching straight towards them, calling out and gesturing with his hand. What they did not see were the two sergeants who crept up behind them. The sentries were quickly overpowered, and within a few minutes the hostages were released.

Having rescued President Jawara's family, Crooke then set about defeating the rest of the rebel force. Rallying around him as many armoured vehicles and trucks as he could find, he then led an all-out assault on the enemy, driving straight to the front door of their command post in the Bakau police centre, where it was believed Western hostages were being held.

What little resistance the rescuers met was quickly subdued by Crooke's firepower. As he and his men crashed into the building expecting to be engaged in deadly combat with a superior force, the rebels were making a run for it through the back door. Within minutes it was all over; the hostages were free and the coup had collapsed. It had taken Crooke and his men just two days.

Compared with the attention that the Iranian Embassy siege had received the previous year, very little interest was taken in what by all accounts seemed to be a story about a small *coup d'état* in a rather insignificant black African state, resolved with the help of neighbouring Senegal.

This of course is the way in which the SAS would much rather operate, in the shadows and away from the public eye. By televising the siege at the embassy the Thatcher government sent a clear signal to the world's terrorists, and that was, 'Don't try it here because we've got the SAS.' When the excitement died down there were some in Hereford who felt the hair rising on the back of their necks, for the techniques used in storming buildings or hijacked aircraft were supposed to rely on secrecy and surprise.

> It goes without saying that every time someone writes their memoirs or details of SAS tactics are revealed, operational procedures can be damaged. Let's not forget that the people who make the rules are just as guilty in this respect as some of the lower ranks. The first story to come out of the Gulf War about McNab's patrol was written by DLB [General Sir Peter de la Billière]. He had the sense to use a certain amount of discretion in the way he told the story, but it didn't take the brain of an Einstein to work out that 'Chris' ['Ryan'] had walked over the border from Iraq to Syria. DLB explained how McNab's patrol had legged it south from the MSR, dog-legged west, then tabbed north going back to the MSR.
>
> Detailing an operational deception plan like that obviously gives an enemy valuable information that he could use to his advantage against Regiment guys in the future. The first bloke to write his memoirs in recent years, 'Soldier I', had a terrible time afterwards and was *persona non grata* as far as the Headshed was concerned. It's the same with 'McNab' and 'Chris Ryan' and anyone else who's tempted to be a film star. Let's just say they're not really the flavour of the month any more, and I doubt if they're still on the Christmas card list either.

Ever changing government attitudes towards foreign powers can lead to some embarrassing situations for those that serve, and today's allies have an annoying habit of becoming tomorrow's enemies. An example of this occurred in 1979 when the Ayatollah Khomeini of Iran appeared to the West, and most especially to the

United States, as being Public Enemy Number One. Khomeini and his supporters had overthrown the monarchy and taken over the country; by 1980, Iran was engaged in a costly and, as it would turn out, long drawn-out war with Saddam Hussein's Iraq. To Western eyes, therefore, Saddam appeared as something of an ally. Few in the West at that time could have foreseen the 'mother of all battles' that Saddam Hussein would promise to wage against an Allied coalition following his invasion of Kuwait on 2 August 1990.

When requests for a 'threat awareness analysis' reached London in 1978, at a time when Khomeini was stirring up trouble in Iran from exile in Paris, no one in the grey world of international commercial security was surprised. Over the years, and initiated by the Regiment's founder, David Stirling, a number of companies had appeared which employed ex-SAS personnel for just this kind of work. As well as advising friendly foreign governments on their security problems, several of these companies also train foreign special forces and provide bodyguards for close-protection duties.

Today there are a handful of such companies, mostly based in London, while several others purporting to employ ex-special forces soldiers use that myth to their advantage. Enterprises employing genuine ex-SAS soldiers include Control Risks, DSL (based in London) and VIP in Surrey.

On this occasion 'the Principal', as SAS bodyguards call the VIP they are guarding, was Saddam Hussein, President of Iraq. Saddam, for somewhat understandable reasons was concerned about his personal safety, and turned to what he and many others see as the world's experts on the subject, the SAS. Requests such as Saddam's are treated with a certain amount of caution by the Ministry of Defence in Whitehall, and careful consideration is always given to the risk of aiding a foreign power in this way.

As British ministers discovered later in the 'Iraqi Supergun' affair, such aid can lead to political embarrassment later on, if or when the story gets out. In this case the request fell into the lap of one London-based security firm, which was only too pleased to offer the specialized services of five retired SAS NCOs. In Baghdad the British team examined Saddam's security and found much to be desired. Not only was his personal bodyguard untrained in the basic techniques of close protection, few, if any, of its members were especially skilled in the use of firearms, particularly handguns.

As is so often the case the bodyguards had convinced themselves, probably by posing in front of the mirror, that they looked the part with their AK-47s and sidearms. The ex-SAS men quickly established a firearms training programme on a specially prepared firing range near Baghdad, and began teaching the President's bodyguards the basics of CQB skills. They closely examined Saddam's travel arrangements and advised him about bulletproof and mine-protected vehicles. Ambush evasion techniques, which involve using the vehicle as a weapon and driving through a killing zone at high speed, were taught, as were other methods for outrunning a potential enemy which the Regiment has developed to a fine art over the years at a training area near Hereford.

Alterations in Baghdad's road layout around the royal palace and government buildings were made, and barriers removed so that Saddam's motorcade could, if necessary, make high-speed turns. During the Gulf crisis twelve years later CIA agents at Langley, Virginia, when asked to present a hypothetical plan for an assassination attempt against Saddam, concluded that the chances of killing him in an ambush would be slim, and that such an attempt could backfire badly if it failed. They recognized the excellent security arrangements surrounding the Iraqi dictator and his personal body-guard, who had apparently paid close attention to the instructions of the ex-SAS advisers. Saddam rarely slept in the same place twice and was constantly on the move, preferring to spend his nights in simple civilian homes rather than his custom-built, bomb-proof shelters. For visits to front-line troops he would travel with his soldiers in plain army trucks, or in a civilian American camper van, of which there were several in Iraq at that time. The only possible way that he could have been killed, the Americans decided, was by obtaining inside information about his exact proposed movements, and the trouble was, these changed constantly. US President George Bush, answering questions in a television interview towards the end of the Gulf War, was asked why the Allies had failed to bomb and kill the Iraqi dictator. Bush tried diplomatically to avoid the subject, but finally admitted that such a task was far from easy. Despite America's formidable array of high-tech military hardware, which included Tomahawk cruise missiles all but capable of turning corners in the back streets of Baghdad, and radar-invisible Stealth bombers, Saddam's security was, unfortunately for the Coalition forces, 'the best in the world'.

The Falklands and Argentina
In the South Atlantic winter of 1982 a number of daring plans were conceived by 'the Kremlin' with a view to bringing the war with Argentina to a swift conclusion. As with all the campaigns in which the Regiment had fought since the Second World War, the possibility of circumventing the traditional and often lack-lustre approach of Britain's generals seemed extremely

appealing. With the tragic loss of twenty of the best and most popular soldiers from D and G Squadrons in a helicopter cross-decking accident at sea on 19 May, there was a strong will amongst the men to hit General Galtieri's forces hard and fast before the Regiment took further casualties.

While members of D Squadron were involved in setting up dangerous covert OPs on the islands, other members of the Regiment were tasked with operations that would bring them face to face with the enemy. When Colonel Michael Rose invited his second-in-command, Major Ian Crooke, to 'do an Entebbe' on the Argentinian airbase at Rio Grande, eyebrows were raised. In that daring 1976 hostage-rescue operation Israeli commandos had flown to Uganda and defeated a gang of pro-Palestinian terrorists who had been given sanctuary by the infamous Idi Amin. With great courage and a clever deception plan, the Israelis, including elements of the elite Golani Brigade, took with them in a Hercules transport plane a Mercedes-Benz limousine identical to Amin's. By using this vehicle they were able to confuse and neutralize the guards in the first critical moments of their operation. They then freed the passengers from the hijacked Air France airliner and flew them safely to Israel, where they were welcomed home as heroes. That operation had impressed even the toughest of SAS soldiers.

The decision was quickly made. Crooke would use two RAF Hercules transport aircraft loaded with B Squadron and flying from Ascension Island, land during the night at Argentina's Rio Grande airbase, destroy its aircraft and kill the pilots. The reason for such a daring attack was simple. Without complete control of the skies, Argentinian Skyhawk and Super Etendard aircraft, the latter armed with French-built Exocet cruise

217

missiles and flown by what one special forces soldier described as 'Latin American racing drivers with lots of balls', were a serious threat to both British ground forces and the Task Force fleet of Royal Navy ships, fleet auxiliaries, merchantmen and passenger vessels. The extent of that threat was seen when the *Atlantic Conveyor*, HMS *Sheffield*, *Sir Galahad* and *Sir Tristram* were either sunk or severely damaged, in some cases with heavy loss of life. Before long, other ships would be lost or damaged in air attacks. Severely hampered by the inability to detect approaching enemy aircraft on radar at the long ranges from which the Super Etendards launched their Exocets, the British Task Force was likely to suffer increasingly heavy casualties. When Prime Minister Margaret Thatcher was told about the plan she was full of enthusiasm. Since the Iranian Embassy siege she had had great confidence in the SAS, and undoubtedly saw the political advantages that such a successful operation could bring to what was seen by many as a rather unpopular war.

With his trusty Fijian NCOs Fred and Tak, Ian Crooke began studying the logistics of the plan, and having consulted his RAF pilots and navigator, quickly realized that problem number one was fuel. The Hercules could reach the Argentinian mainland more than 4,000 miles away and land, but even with in-flight refuelling, if anything went wrong they would have little chance of getting back to Ascension Island.

Alternative landing sites did not exist within range, the only possible one being an airbase in Chile, but political diplomacy prevented Britain from compromising Chile's neutrality in the war. The second slightly worrying aspect of the job was that Rio Grande was guarded by an unknown force of Argentinian infantrymen and an anti-aircraft battalion equipped with ground-to-air missiles. During a detailed briefing on Ascension Island members of B Squadron did their best to make light of the affair, but it has to be admitted that, for most of them, the operation had all the hallmarks of a suicide mission. Even if the Argentinian anti-aircraft guns and missiles failed to shoot them down on the approach, it seemed most unlikely that they would be able to hold their own against a fighting force outnumbering them by probably more than ten to one. In their uncomfortable quarters on Ascension Island, B Squadron checked their weapons and grenades one last time, and glanced nervously at their watches. A few who had experience of the long and deafening Hercules C130 flights had brought hammocks with them which they planned to tie to the aircraft's bulkheads. For the older veterans the only thing to do at times like this was to get some zeds (forty winks).

Men who had not already 'blacked-up' with the Max Factor camouflage cream were taking care of this final detail while Crooke checked his maps and conferred with Hereford. B Squadron's sergeant major arrived at the men's quarters and gave the order to load magazines and prime grenades. The raid was on. Everyone moved out to the transport vehicles a few hundred metres away from the Hercules. And then suddenly it happened: 'Abort the mission.' An intelligence assessment of the situation had finally convinced the planners in the Headshed, the Joint Operations Centre (JOC), and ministers in the Cabinet Office Briefing Room (COBRA), that this raid really was going to be suicide and that the repercussions could be disastrous.

Feelings of relief were soon followed by a wave of disappointment as B Squadron was stood down. To counter the threat from the mainland, something had to be done, and if an Entebbe-style raid was not feasible, perhaps there was an alternative. An operation was planned which involved eight SAS men and the crew of a Royal Navy Sea King helicopter flown by two intrepid Fleet Air Arm lieutenants. The plan was to put the small team on to the Argentinian mainland to monitor the movements of enemy aircraft from their coastal bases at either Rio Grande or Rio Gallegos, both a short distance from the Chilean border and either side of the Magellan Straits.

Owing to Chile's neutrality in the Falklands conflict it was of vital importance that whatever covert and unlawful activities the SAS got up to on its territory, they would have to be deniable and carried out in the utmost secrecy. Whether agents from the Secret Intelligence Service (MI6) working out of the British Embassy in Chile's capital Santiago played any part in the operation is open to conjecture, but it seems unlikely that there was not some collusion between them and the Headshed at the time.

On 20 May a Sea King HC Mark 4 helicopter, ZA290 (and not a Mark 5 as has been suggested by other authors), belonging to 846 Commando Squadron was discovered by Chilean authorities in a field overlooking the Magellan Straits, about ten nautical miles south of Punta Arenas, the only town with a commercial airport in the remote Brunswick Peninsula. The back of the helicopter was broken and the cabin interior had been severely burnt. Eye-witnesses who went to what appeared to be the crash site thought the damage might have been caused by an explosion, perhaps an exploding grenade. Not long after the discovery, the three-man crew, Lieutenants Richard Hutchings, Alan Bennett and Leading Aircrewman Peter Imrie appeared, having gone to ground in what strongly resembled a classic downed-aircraft survival scenario. What appeared unusual to the Chilean authorities was that no distress flares had been seen, and no 'Mayday' messages had been sent on the international distress frequency. Any pilot who has been trained to survive and wants to be rescued knows at least half a dozen ways to attract attention.

The crew, although rather cold and weary, clearly knew how to look after themselves. It was hardly surprising. Lieutenant Hutchings was a qualified military survival instructor, and as is perfectly normal with all such personnel, his crewmates had attended survival courses during which they had learnt to make shelters, build signal fires and live off the land. So where did they come from and what were they doing? At a press conference in Santiago some time later, the trio stuck to a story that they had been on a sea patrol when their helicopter had suffered engine failure caused by adverse weather conditions. The territory at the southern tip of South America with its many small and barren islands has long been the subject of disputes between Chile and Argentina. The area flanking the Magellan Straits which belongs to Chile would have made an ideal entry point for the low-flying Sea King, but the crew were noncommittal about where exactly they had come from. The helicopter's normal operating range of 664 nautical miles meant that its crew, assuming they had flown to the mainland from the Task Force fleet, would only have had a short time in which to carry out their mission.

If one assumes – and of course when discussing SAS operations one can assume very little – that the take-off was made from a ship on the edge of Britain's 200-nautical-mile total exclusion zone, just under a third of the Sea King's fuel would have been used up before it reached the mainland. That would leave fuel for a maximum of 464 nautical miles for carrying out its mission, enough in theory to return to its mother ship. However, the Falklands campaign saw the introduction of two revolutionary procedures which dramatically changed the fighting capabilities of Britain's Special Forces.

The first was helicopter in-flight refuelling (HIFR), an innovative system which enabled Sea King and other helicopters to refuel without landing. During one operation in the Falklands, a Sea King from 826 Commando Squadron succeeded in staying airborne for a record ten hours and twenty minutes. HIFR required a pumping station, filter module and fuel from either a ship at sea, a land base, or perhaps even a submarine.

The other dramatic advance in covert operations was the pilots' use of passive night-vision (PNV) goggles. At the start of the war the Fleet Air Arm's 846 Squadron had five Sea King HC Mark 4s dedicated to special forces operations with night-vision goggle (NVG) compatible cockpit-lighting systems. Just before leaving England each crew was issued with a small supply of the latest American Anvis night-vision goggles, but they had little opportunity to try them out. Being able to contour-fly in the dark at low level now gave the SAS and SBS a dramatic tactical advantage.

Each of the night flights to insert covert patrols was flown by two pilots and a crewman, the man with the controls wearing Anvis third-generation NVGs, with the second pilot and crewman using the slightly less sensitive second-generation models. On their voyage down to the Falklands, one of 846 Squadron's Sea Kings was lost in an accident, reducing the special forces-dedicated aircraft to four. During the conflict these four Sea Kings flew an incredible 736 covert sorties, either to insert SAS or SBS teams or to re-supply them. Flying 'by the seat of their pants' at night 15 metres above the ground requires nerves of steel, and the SAS personnel who flew with the young Fleet Air Arm pilots came greatly to admire and respect their coolness under stress.

Operating from the anti-submarine carrier HMS *Hermes*, which like other ships in the fleet was at risk from Argentinian aircraft, 846 Squadron's SF-dedicated Sea Kings were used for troop insertion during Operation 'Prelim'. This daring raid, a few days before the Chilean adventure, was probably the single most successful SAS operation of the war. On the night of 11 May, three Sea Kings took off from *Hermes*, which was positioned more than an hour's flying time from the target, Pebble Island, an Argentinian airbase on the northern coast of East Falkland. On board were most of D Squadron. In the early hours of the next day, the SAS men mounted a devastating raid on the island's airstrip and destroyed eleven enemy aircraft. After the operation, which took five days to complete and resulted in only two SAS casualties, HMS *Hermes* then made a high-speed dash towards the South American mainland. How far she got before launching the Chile-bound Sea King is open to speculation.

As has already been mentioned, on the night of 19 May, two days before the British landings at San Carlos, the Regiment lost twenty of its best men, including the two who had been wounded at Pebble Island, in a tragic cross-decking accident as members of D Squadron, elements of G, and a handful of unbadged attached headquarters personnel were transferring from HMS *Hermes* to the assault ship HMS *Intrepid*. The 846 Squadron Sea King HC Mk4, ZA294, crashed into the Atlantic when a seabird, thought to have been a giant petrel, flew into its tail rotor. News of the accident sent a wave of grief right through the Regiment. As Hereford mourned its dead and missing men, on the mainland of South America the Chile operation was already under way.

From the most westerly point of the Falkland Islands to the entrance of Chile's Magellan Straits is around 350 nautical miles (NM), or a little over three hours' Sea King flying time. If HMS *Hermes* was somewhere between this distance and the total exclusion zone's 200-nautical-mile limit, this means that the helicopter's operational range over Chile was, as has been said, at best 464 NM, or at worst, 350 NM. Punta Arenas, where the helicopter finally came to rest, is 108 NM from Rio Gallegos and 121 NM from Rio Grande. To land near both targets and finish up at Punta Arenas means flying for 229 NM at the very least. If we discount the possibility of HIFR from a land station (there is no land between the Falklands and Chile), then unless this task was undertaken by a submarine, Sea King ZA290 would only have three or at most four hours to deliver its team before the fuel ran out. This means that by the time the helicopter reached the Magellan Straits after flying 300 NM in a minimum of two hours forty minutes, there was not enough fuel left for the return trip. There was, however, just enough time to drop off an SAS reconnaissance team close to, or just inside, the Chile–Argentina frontiers. Having deposited them within walking distance of either (or both) Rio Gallegos or Rio Grande, the helicopter would have just sufficient fuel to make a rushed landing 10 NM south of Punta Arenas.

But why Punta Arenas? The answer is simple, and clear to anyone who cares to study a map. Ditching the Sea King in the extremely cold waters of the Magellan Straits, which would have been the best way of making it disappear, thus avoiding a diplomatic incident, would have been potentially suicidal for the three-man crew. The landing site they chose instead is almost equidistant from the two separate Chile–Argentina borders, behind which were located the target airbases. By lying up and keeping out of sight for as long as they could, or until the risk of compromising the mission had ended, the Sea King's crew gave the SAS valuable breathing space, time in which to set up their OPs.

What actually happened on that daring operation shows the importance of the mission, and the incontrovertible courage of its participants. The threat of air attack by Argentinian Super Etendards on the British fleet just before the main landings posed an almost insuperable problem for the planners, but the SAS, who are no strangers to near-impossible tasks, decided to have a go. Aboard helicopter ZA290 as it raced across the Atlantic in the dark there were eleven men, including its three-man Fleet Air Arm crew. The Sea King had been stripped of all but the most necessary equipment, and beneath its floor was enough plastic explosive to turn it in seconds into an exploding fireball. The eight SAS men on board were sitting on a flying bomb.

As they approached the enemy coast the inevitable happened. Sensors in the helicopter told the crew that an Argentinian IFF ground radar station had locked on to them, and the pilots were forced to take dramatic action to avoid ground-to-air missile batteries. Seeking sanctuary in a deep valley, the Sea King flew at high speed a few feet above the ground as the crew tried desperately to locate their pre-determined drop-off point inside Argentina. The target for the eight-man SAS team was Rio Grande, and the helicopter crew's task was to get them as close to that area as possible. Realizing they had been spotted and already running short of fuel, the patrol's commander agreed with the pilots that their only option was to drop the patrol just inside the Chilean border and destroy the helicopter.

Under the cover of darkness and using PNV goggles, the pilot made a rapid landing, said his hurried goodbyes to the SAS team, who had set the explosive charges in the helicopter, and disappeared into the night. By morning the eight-man patrol was deep inside Argentina and concealed in lying-up positions. Using the well-practised technique of moving at night and hiding during the day, they headed for the airstrip at Rio Grande, but soon discovered that the enemy's airbase and its surrounding area were swarming with Argentinian troops. Any attempt at penetrating the strongly defended perimeter was clearly suicidal, and having reported the situation to Hereford using high-speed Morse, the patrol's commander eventually ordered the team to pull out.

Meanwhile elements of B Squadron, who had recently arrived from Ascension Island by parachuting into the cold waters of the Atlantic, had transferred to one of the Royal Navy's smaller submarines, HMS *Onyx*, and were heading for the Magellan Straits. On board they carried inflatable Zodiac craft, and on their journey they practised night launches, floating away from the submerging submarine. Their task, like their comrades who had been inserted by helicopter, was to observe and then organize an attack on Rio Grande. But after almost a week, and by then submerged in the Magellan Straits, the submarine received a signal informing them that Argentina had surrendered and that there were white flags flying over Port Stanley. The war was over. Clearly, the task of destroying the Super Etendard threat had proved impossible for even the SAS, and this taught a valuable lesson to the planners in Whitehall. It is one thing to ask your special forces to attempt the suicidal, another to accomplish the impossible.

When the wreckage of the helicopter had finally been discovered, the enemy had wasted valuable time, and deployed key personnel to little purpose, to work out which, if either, of the two airbases had been targeted for covert surveillance. By the time they had mobilized sufficient forces to mount a search around the bases, the SAS men had vanished.

The Sea King aircrew received the Distinguished Service Cross (Lieutenants Hutchings and Bennett) and the Distinguished Service Medal (Leading Aircrewman Imrie). Awards to the SAS men who participated in the operation have not been made public. Interestingly, the Sea King HC Mark 4, ZA290 Commando was the first of its type to be built by Westland, and therefore the oldest. Its final clandestine flight was perhaps a fitting end to a long and noble career. Exactly how the mainland team managed to escape, nobody knows, apart from the participants of the operation and a few Chileans who helped to get them back.

Bosnia

The fact that the SAS had been operating in the bloody civil war in the former Yugoslavia will come as no great surprise to the general public, but the depth of their involvement has been a well-kept secret. For the first time since the Second World War, the Regiment had been drawn into a conflict on the European mainland which, until a short time ago, political commentators and United Nations observers believed might spread out of control like a forest fire. That the war was contained despite enormous human tragedy says much for the work of brave UN peacekeepers and civilian volunteers from non-governmental organizations (NGOs) who risked, and often gave, their lives to help the innocent victims of the conflict. Operating in the shadows of this bitter war and unseen by television cameras were the SAS, watching and occasionally fighting against the rival factions.

When British soldiers began their United Nations peacekeeping mission in Bosnia it quickly became apparent that unless commanders on the ground were prepared to use force, the Serb, Croat, and Bosnian militias would enjoy their anarchic freedom throughout the country, killing and destroying at will as US soldiers looked on. There appeared to be among many of the fighters, according to some who have served there, very little logic, only bitterness with its roots buried in the memory of previous generations. For some of the British special forces soldiers who went to Bosnia, this was a conflict, albeit on a much larger scale, not so very far removed from what many of them had experienced in Northern Ireland. The psychopathic hatred among some of the fighters and the indiscriminate massacre of civilians were factors that demanded great professionalism and self-control from the soldiers serving there.

The SAS's involvement in the war began in its early stages when Ministry of Defence planners in London and the defence attaché in Belgrade began studying the dangerous implications of the growing conflict. Officers at Hereford's Headshed, who pride themselves on keeping abreast of current affairs, closely monitored developments as the first British Army contingents began arriving in Vitez in the autumn of 1992. Initially the soldiers from the Cheshire Regiment seemed to be in little danger in their UN observer role, but within days of their arrival they found themselves pinned down under the cross-fire of warring Bosnian army and Croatian forces. Despite strict orders from Whitehall not to get involved or take sides, the Cheshires opened fire in self-defence, and this incident became the turning point in British peacekeeping operations.

A special forces soldier who was in Beirut during Britain's UN operations there in 1983 recalled:

It takes a lot of guts perched behind the sandbags in a sangar [a breastwork of stones, sandbags etc.] with a pair of binos listening to shells and mortar rounds passing overhead, not only because your job is to count the rounds each side lobs at one another, but also because you're expecting their bombs and shells to fall short, and that means on top of you. If the political will is there, which it rarely is, you can usually take them [the aggressors] out without much trouble, but the support must be there, otherwise you're dead.

Whether by accident or design, and only history will tell, in the case of Bosnia the support was there, though perhaps only reluctantly. Britain's political establishment, and especially its successive defence ministers, were afraid of standing alone and getting bogged down in an unprofitable war without the firm support of Britain's allies, and that, when the chips were down, meant America. A recently retired NCO said:

> The big difference between Bosnia and Belfast is that the yellow card rules really don't apply and you're not obliged to account for every shot you fire. This was much more like Iraq, more like a real war as a soldier knows it. A lot of the time convoys were getting ambushed and innocent civilian aid workers were taking casualties. It was only right that someone from our side occasionally went in amongst the bad guys and sorted them out. They had to be taught a lesson. If you shoot at us we're going to shoot back, and something you're going to learn fast is that we can do it better than you.

Before long it became abundantly clear to all the fighting factions in Bosnia that the British Army was determined to enforce the deliveries of aid to areas under its control, unlike some of the other UN contingents which opted for less forceful responses to intimidation by militiamen who routinely blocked supply routes and searched and turned back aid convoys. It is conservatively estimated that during the first two years of British

Army operations in Bosnia at Vitez, Tomislavgrad and Gornji Vakuf, a minimum of 100 militiamen from the Croat and Muslim sides were killed in exchanges of fire with British soldiers.

In January 1994 General Sir Michael Rose became the first British officer to take command of UNPRO-FOR, and with him he brought a breath of fresh air to a degenerating situation in the country; he also brought SAS ideas. This was the man who had led the Regiment through the Falklands war, and two years before that had directed the lifting of the Iranian Embassy siege. As far as Rose was concerned, the time for compromise had passed and all the fighting factions in Bosnia had to be brought to heel.

Earlier SAS reconnaissance missions had provided the new commander and his staff with valuable information about the strengths and dispositions of enemy forces, and within days of Rose's arrival an entire squadron was operating in the country. Working alongside them were elements of 264 Signals Regiment and some of the DET men from Northern Ireland operations.[2] Their target was Gorazde where the inhabitants, cut off from the main supply route from Sarajevo, were struggling to survive under a constant barrage of Serb shells. In the mountainous countryside the only way that supplies could reach the townsfolk was by a dangerous cross-country route through Serb positions which led to the deaths of many civilians who tried. SAS four- and eight-man patrols, moving under the cover of darkness and lying up in hides in the day, soon got to know this region well.

In the spring of 1994 they mounted intelligence-gathering operations to monitor the locations of Serb artillery and mortar positions, their command and control structure, and ammunition dumps.

[2] See Chapter Seven: She Who Dares Wins.

Rose and UNPROFOR were target hunting. The General knew of only one way to stop a siege like this one. Hit them hard with precision air strikes, but in order to do that successfully and without causing needless innocent casualties, you had to have good men on the ground who could guide in the attack just as the SAS has done inside Iraq.

In mid-April two of Rose's men operating as part of an eight-man patrol were wounded, one seriously, when they were caught up in a Serb attack. Attempts to extract the patrol proved impossible. Finally a decision was taken by the six remaining soldiers to fight their way out. One informed source said:

> Apparently after Rose's requests for close air support to get them out were turned down by Mr Akashi the UN negotiator they legged it cross-country towards Sarajevo avoiding the fighting around Gorazde. That's a fair distance. During the journey they ran straight into a Serb patrol of about a dozen men. There was no way they were going to be able to talk their way out of that so they just opened up on them, straight in and they fought their way through. Luckily there was no real contest, it was all over in a couple of minutes, and they [the SAS patrol] accounted for the entire Serb patrol.

The two wounded men were treated by Serbian medics but unfortunately one of them died from his injuries. The escapers eventually arrived in Sarajevo and reported back to General Rose, having completed their hazardous journey by dodging Serb positions under the cover of darkness. These behind-the-lines operations continued throughout 1994 with the SAS using methods of insertion into Serb areas that occasionally caused embarrassment to the United Nations. Suggestions that SAS teams operated in the conflict by driving around in civilian ambulances as a method of gathering intelligence can neither be confirmed nor denied by this author, and it will no doubt be some time before the full story of Britain's special forces' operations is made public. Suffice it to say that David Stirling, who had once observed during the Second World War that 'you could easily drive through an enemy position if you've got the balls to do it', would have been proud of the men that operated there. What is clear is that once again the SAS was deeply and very secretly involved in a very dirty war.

Central and South America

Since the late 1980s the SAS has carried out a number of covert anti-drug operations in support of friendly Central and South American governments, often in co-operation with US Green Berets and the US Drug Enforcement Agency (DEA). When Sergeant Timothy Cowley, a thirty-three-year-old clerk who worked at the British Embassy in Bogotá, Colombia, was kidnapped by guerrillas from the Revolutionary Armed Forces of Colombia (FARC) during a bird-watching expedition, a small SAS team backed up by Colombian police and special forces was deployed to organize the search for him. During Cowley's 112 days of captivity, he was held in Tolima province deep in the Andean mountains, but following a series of tip-offs and some skilful tracking by the rescuers, he was finally abandoned by his captors, who fled into the hills. The training of indigenous anti-terrorist and drug enforcement teams is likely to continue in this area, as well as other parts of the world where drug barons enjoy the freedom to carry on their evil trade.

ELEVEN

THE SURVIVORS

Where do SAS men go when their military careers are over? One thing that is certain is that very few reach retirement age without showing the physical or mental scars brought on by a lifetime's hard soldiering. To survive at all is, in itself, an achievement considering the nature of their work, the risks being perhaps comparable to those of a professional mountaineer who, having climbed Ben Nevis in his teens, is attempting the north face of the Eiger or Everest in his twenties. Apart from a few 1990s soldiers who grew up in an age where heavy smoking and drinking had become less acceptable, one might be inclined to believe that a lot of them subscribed to the 'live hard, die young, make a good-looking corpse' theory. Perhaps this is all part of the hard-man image of the Regiment's soldiers that has been portrayed over the years, not necessarily by the soldiers themselves, although it does not displease them, but rather by those who observe them. In short, they have become a loyal and controllable force, Britain's last line of defence in an unpredictable and increasingly dangerous world.

What is often overlooked is the plain courage it takes to accomplish dangerous missions where the chances of coming out alive are slim. Leonard Cheshire, VC, the charismatic and highly decorated Second World War bomber pilot, once described courage as belonging to one of two categories: a) men with acute imagination who realized they would probably die but who forced themselves to go on; and b) men who, though intelligent, could shut their minds off through imagination and carry on without acute forebodings of the future. One SAS man said during the Falklands War that he and his comrades-in-arms strongly resented being portrayed as psychopathic killers by the media, ready to be released as if from a cage by the government of the day for use against the country's foes. While never denying the fact that they are highly skilled in many different methods of killing, including the use of their bare hands, most would rather be admired for their powers of lateral thinking, their individual skills, and their humour.

The financial rewards for the service they give to the country are limited, and it is quite rare to meet an SAS man who has served a lifetime in the Regiment, perhaps leaving as a senior NCO, who does not have financial worries. Consequently the notion of taking up private security work when they leave seems attractive to many, and a number of reputable firms exist which employ such men on normally very specific short contract jobs. Lists of suitable candidates for these assignments are not easily obtainable.

The ex-SAS circuit is just as discreet in its actions as that of the fully fledged regiment, and only reveals what it cares to let outsiders see. At least one modern database, run by a retired member, can inform potential clients about the availability of suitable candidates, but such clients' references are always thoroughly checked before any actual recruiting takes place. This will sometimes mean a discreet vetting of the customer's standing in the community through unofficial contacts in

Whitehall who may include MI5 or MI6, or foreign agencies such as the CIA. This sometimes leads to a 'gypsy warning' about a particular individual or company who might present a risk either to national security or Britain's long-term interests.

Some members, on leaving 22 SAS Regiment, join the elite R Squadron,[1] a highly experienced reserve force which contains among its ranks a number of the most highly qualified and longest-serving veterans. These are often men who have left the army relatively early in their careers, but whose valuable experience can be called upon in times of emergency, such as happened during the Gulf War. These men are by no means the standard Territorial or 'weekend soldiers' kept in reserve for a potential Third World War, but rather an elite within an elite.

One of the first people to sense that retiring or injured SAS soldiers might fall into the unemployment trap after their army service was David Stirling. Like himself, many veterans had fought courageously for their country and had then been left to fend for themselves, often living on a small army or disablement pension. In 1967 Stirling formed a company called Watchguard, based in Guernsey, and soon ex-members were training the elite forces of a number of foreign countries with the tacit approval of Her Majesty's Government. This arrangement did not only offer the men employment, it also introduced political deniability into the equation. An ex-SAS man who dies overseas while engaged in some remote conflict can quite easily be dismissed as having died through his own misadventure, even if a 'grey suit' in Whitehall has discreetly encouraged his participation. Such events are, however, fairly

[1] In 1996 R Squadron was re-named L Detachment after David Stirling's unit of 'Originals' in the Second World War.

rare. Someone who knows the business of special forces operations is usually quite capable of looking after himself in all but the most disastrous of cases.

Specialist assignments for ex-members can sometimes take them to the wildest places on earth, and in 1981, shortly after the Soviet army's entry into Afghanistan, a daring operation was carried out by two British ex-soldiers, Sammy Evans and Phil Sassarego. The former had served for several years in the Regiment's A Squadron. Working for the CIA through a London-based intermediary, they succeeded in joining up with a mujaheddin force in Pakistan, then crossed the Afghan frontier at night. Once inside Afghanistan they trekked for miles on a journey that took them across the south-western slopes of the Hindu Kush mountain range until they finally reached their prey, which was not a Soviet base or armoured column, but a crashed Hind helicopter.

The CIA was especially interested in the helicopter's titanium armour, and so, armed with a chainsaw, which the retired A Squadron man used more commonly in his employment with the Forestry Commission in Wales, the pair sliced off a portion of the helicopter's skin. After a number of hair-raising adventures on their return journey in a country where mujaheddin inter-factional rivalries could be just as life-threatening to a foreigner as the Soviet and Afghan government armies, they managed to deliver the armour and return safely to London. Such dangerous work, although highly paid by a soldier's standards, usually pays a fraction of what most civilian company directors might expect to earn in a month.

The war in Afghanistan attracted two other SAS veterans, but instead of carrying arms, both carried television cameras. Producing news footage in such a hostile environment where the terrain would defeat all but the toughest individual called for a very specialized and hardy operator. Nick Downie, who had served in B Squadron before becoming a cameraman in the Rhodesian war, was the first to venture into the Hindu Kush carrying a television camera. His documentary films of mujaheddin guerrillas in combat against Soviet troops were seen around the world during the 1980s, though he soon discovered that filming them in action was a very haphazard and risky business. The guerrillas' tactics were unlike anything the ex-SAS man had ever seen before, and although not short of courage, their attacks were rarely well planned or skilfully executed.

Andy Skrzpkowiak,[2] a charismatic ex-paratrooper and RTU'd member of A Squadron's HALO Troop who had fought with the Regiment in Oman, and whose Polish refugee parents had settled in London after the Second World War, followed in Downie's footsteps and worked as a freelance cameraman on assignments for the BBC and other television networks. He quickly identified the toughest and most skilled of the mujaheddin groups operating in the Panjshir Valley led by the courageous Ahmed Shah Massood, and the two men soon became close friends. Massood's Jamiyat-Islami group carried out daring hit-and-run raids against Soviet and Afghan government forces and, by 1986, the main Soviet supply route through the Salang Pass into Afghanistan became a virtual no-go area. Whenever Massood's men launched an attack, Skrzypkowiak, known to his friends as 'Popski', would place himself in the front-line assault group to film deadly scenes of close combat, on one occasion lying hidden in a ditch beside an RPG-7 operator as Soviet tanks and BMPs rolled past him a few metres away on the road. Skrzypkowiak

[2] Contrary to some published reports, Skrzypkowiak was never a member of 21 SAS Regiment. He served in the 1st Battalion, Parachute Regiment, then 22 SAS Regiment.

was so close that he could almost touch their wheels. As the RPG-7 was fired at the lead tank, causing it to explode, he filmed the battle with Kalashnikov rounds cracking around his head. Skrzypkowiak said that filming the Afghan war was more dangerous that anything he had ever encountered in the SAS.

In October 1987, during one of his frequent visits to the war, and shortly after filming American Stinger missiles being fired for the first time against Soviet aircraft, he returned to Afghanistan, only to be murdered in his sleep by a renegade group linked to Gulbuddin Hekmatyar's Hezbi-Islami faction, sworn enemies of Massood's Jamiyat group. Details of Skrzypkowiak's murder were only revealed following an undercover operation led by the retired second-in-command of 22 SAS, Lieutenant-Colonel (as he had become) Ian Crooke, who at that time was a director of David Stirling's London-based security company, KAS. The Regiment's founder took a special interest in Skrzypkowiak's fate, on one occasion saying that he reminded him of his fellow desert warrior, the heroic Paddy Mayne.

Popski had planned to cross the Afghan frontier with a Jamiyat–Islami group from the border town of Chitral, in Pakistan, but when the armed escort failed to turn up, he decided to make the journey with a trusted guide named Oskabeer, whom he knew from previous visits.

After crossing the border and trekking for several days through the mountains of Nuristan, the two men were ambushed by a dozen Hezbi-Islami guerrillas on horseback who had previously bushwhacked and robbed a French humanitarian medical team. The gang immediately attacked and beat up Oskabeer, and when one of the group tried to take Skrzypkowiak's Aaton television camera, the SAS veteran lashed out at the Kalashnikov-wielding thief, knocking him to the ground. During the hours that followed, Skrzypkowiak, who never carried a weapon on his assignments, somehow managed to escape from his captors and made off on foot in the direction of the Panjshir Valley. The horsemen caught up with him at the top of the Kantiwar Pass which was some twenty kilometres away, and with little cover to hide in and realizing his escape had failed, he had no option but to let them lead him at gunpoint back down the mountain. As night fell, the exhausted Skrzypkowiak, who had walked most of the day in a rarefied atmosphere at high altitude carrying a heavy bergen before making his escape, and had run uphill almost twenty kilometres, was ordered by his captors to bed down for the night. Although holding him prisoner, they assured him that the next day he would be allowed to leave a free man.

In his sleeping-bag beside a low stone wall, he dozed off. Later that night, six members of the gang silently crept up on the sleeping cameraman and dropped a massive boulder on his head, killing him instantly. Their murderous act accomplished, the gang carried Popski's body, still in its sleeping-bag, across a river and hid their victim in a cave. A group of playing children discovered the body some time later, and when Kantiwar villagers examined the sleeping-bag, they found a bayonet from a Kalashnikov rifle beside the body. Skrzypkowiak, it appeared, had somehow managed to steal the bayonet and was clearly planning another escape, but it seems he never had the chance.

The Stinger anti-aircraft missiles that he had filmed on his previous trip a few months before were part of a consignment delivered by the CIA by a roundabout route which passed through Saudi Arabia. The more moderate Jamiyat-Islami faction which received them put these missiles to good use, although they had some difficulty at first in making them work effectively. When the missiles' teething problems had been resolved the effect was dramatic. Now denied control of the Afghan skies, Soviet helicopters and bombers were put at serious risk, and within a few months of their appearance in the Afghan war, Soviet forces began their withdrawal. More than any other weapon, this frighteningly effective piece of military hardware, once in the hands of competent operators, had defeated a superpower.

The stubbornness of the Afghan people, who refused to admit defeat at the hands of a heavily equipped aggressor, proved that a small, dedicated band of fighters can win a modern war. Where are those Stingers now? Since the end of the war against the Soviet-backed regime in Afghanistan there has not been a single day of peace, and the internecine fighting between rival Muslim factions in that country is likely to continue for a long time. Modern and devastatingly effective weapons like Stinger could quite easily turn up in the hands of a terrorist anywhere in the world, to be used to bring down military or civilian aircraft. Whether the CIA was right to supply them to the mujaheddin at all is a difficult question to answer, but such covert, if well-intentioned, operations can so very easily backfire.

Bodyguarding the family of a wealthy Arab sheikh in London today pays ex-SAS men around £200 a day before tax. On top of this amount there is a tradition of baksheesh, a special thank you from the principal[3] they are guarding in the form of lavish jewellery, watches being a favourite, or cash at the end of each engagement. Such jobs may last through the summer months when the oppressive heat in the Arabian Gulf drives

[3] The principal – bodyguards' terminology for a VIP they are protecting.

many members of Arab ruling families to the cooler climes of Europe.

Again, it was Stirling who began this tradition of SAS-style protection for visiting Arab heads of state and their families, who today own vast estates in Scotland and the Home Counties. In the Highlands of Scotland, affluent Arabian princes now enjoy the field sports once the preserve of the British aristocracy, and more than one Arabian leader today owns a priceless collection of racehorses and a large part of London's exorbitantly priced Mayfair.

The men who are selected to guard these and other similar high-risk targets have all completed SAS courses that teach bodyguard teams (BG teams) techniques of threat assessment (learning through acquired intelligence and observation to judge levels of threat), convoy protection (sticking close to to the VIP's vehicle and travelling tactically), and evasive vehicle manoeuvres. The result of their endeavours is rarely seen or spoken about, proving, as the Diplomatic and Royalty Protection Groups do each day, their low-key efficiency. An ex-special forces soldier who spends his summer months bodyguarding a royal family from one of the Gulf states says:

The whole point about being a good bodyguard in an anti-terrorist scenario is avoiding being noticed. If you roar up with a screech of brakes and you're halfway out of the car before it stops, that's you compromised. It's much better to move the principal in a nondescript vehicle instead of a limousine if you can persuade him away from the limo. Of course some of them want the comfort and prestige of a flash car which only makes your job more difficult. Armoured and bomb-resistant vehicles are a definite asset, but your job is to avoid the threat, not confront it. In Northern Ireland we'd sometimes use decoy convoys to move a high-profile target around, slip the VIP out the back when the eyes and ears of the locals were fixed elsewhere. Most of it is common sense, but some of the best BG men and women, well, you just wouldn't notice them at all as they look so nondescript and blend easily into the background. Most ex-soldiers who want BG work have to be retrained unless they've completed one of the Regiment's special courses. They've usually watched too many films with G-men wearing sunglasses and earplugs who talk into their cufflinks. Most of it is very boring, long hours and hotel rooms with heavy planning sessions, teamwork and missed meals. It's a good living if you're not prone to stomach ulcers and don't mind being bossed around and fired by some jumped-up little Arab prince. Luckily most of the jobs which pay well don't last too long.

Sometimes the routine of bodyguarding turns to monotony, and the temptation to branch out into business ventures becomes irresistible, but success for most who try is usually rare. For those ex-troopers and NCOs who have concentrated on developing a particular trade or following a specific interest, the future can be bright, but in most cases the shock of becoming a civvy after years wearing camouflage is dramatic. The situation is, of course, slightly different for officers, who may blend into the cut-throat world of business more easily. One such officer was appointed head of an international airline's security, while another became a 'name' at Lloyd's and lost a fortune.

Inevitably there are the drifters and the 'wild cards', individuals who some might associate with the frustrated ex-soldier epitomized by Sylvester Stallone in the original *Rambo* film epic, but no SAS soldier would ever accept such a comparison. To most, Stallone's character, like most actors who play similar roles, lacks military credibility, and Rambo has certainly never been seen at the movies running up a mountain, bent double and carrying a colossal SAS bergen. Nor does he ever seem to run short of ammunition, which is unusual when one counts the number of rounds he fires. Special Air Service veterans are perhaps the most critical war-movie watchers on the planet, but that said, most would much rather curl up in front of a wildlife film or a documentary about trout fishing, or even better, get out in the fresh air and catch the trout themselves.

If depression sets in, which is not uncommon for men who have sometimes lost close friends in distant places in horrific circumstances or who have killed large numbers of their country's enemies in the heat of battle, there is a tendency to solve the problem with the bottle. Which bottle usually depends on what particular alcohol is available, though one ex-trooper had a particular penchant for dark rum, which in moments of depression he would gulp down like spring water. The SAS's potent G-10 (quartermaster's stores) rum ration was a particular favourite on cold nights in faraway places and would ensure a good night's sleep to many serving on overseas operations. That particular ex-trooper once drank too much of it in London's West End before trying to take the Underground home in the early hours of a summer morning.

Discovering that the last tube train had already departed, he set about trying to open the station's grille gates with his bare hands, oblivious to the fact that the station was closed and there would be a long wait before the service started again. When challenged by a policeman on his beat, the man told the PC to mind his own business and went on with the task of forcing the gate.

As the policeman started to restrain the offender with the usual, 'I think you'd better come along with me, sonny,' the ex-trooper defended himself. In less than a second, a dazed and prostrate officer of the law was crawling on his hands and knees up the station's steps, nursing his injuries and calling for help on his personal radio. When backup arrived (the ex-trooper had made no attempt to leave the scene and by now had succeeded in opening the gates) a running battle ensued with several policemen sustaining black eyes and bruises.

Eventually, overpowered by a superior force and persuaded to come quietly, the culprit was delivered to the cell complex in one of London's West End police stations. The duty sergeant, was, however, unable and unwilling to risk more casualties (this was before the days of long-handled police batons and CS gas), and the culprit spent the rest of the night in the corridor. The next morning he faced the local magistrate, but by this time the accused had made friends with most of the walking-wounded policemen in the station, and on hearing that he had served in the SAS the charges against him were reduced. On that occasion, he was bound over to keep the peace and let off with a small fine, though his fists and temper would still cause him problems in later life.

While many who have served in the Regiment grow old quietly with their memories, reunions of SAS veterans have a habit of turning into extremely alcoholic affairs. A few years ago during one such get-together at the Duke of York's Barracks in Chelsea, and after several hours of heavy drinking, a still-serving NCO organized accommodation for those who thought it wiser not to drive home.

Sleeping-bags or 'maggots' were laid out on the floor of the drill hall and gradually, one by one, they were filled by a dozen or more very drunken and elderly men.

The next morning when an orderly came in to offer strong coffee and Alka-Seltzer, he was horrified to discover that one veteran had died peacefully during the night. The police were called, and during their careful examination of the corpse it was found that the man had been wearing a wig to hide his baldness. When the police and representatives of the Regiment called at his home, they discovered firstly that the man had lived alone and was a bit of a recluse, and then to their shock that the property had been carefully booby-trapped to discourage intruders.

It was a lucky escape for the group who called at the man's flat, for someone could easily have been killed just by opening the door. For several years following the incident, the veteran's wig held a place of honour over the bar in the 21 Regiment SAS sergeants' mess.

The SAS Regimental Association, which is run by retired soldiers for the welfare of their colleagues, organizes events, trips and reunions for veterans and keeps them up to date with news of their comrades and their families. More than anything it tries to help those who have fallen by the wayside because of circumstances beyond their control. Illness and suffering caused by old battle injuries can render a once-fit man completely drained and unable to cope. The Association strives to help such men, and is also on hand to comfort the families of those who fail to 'beat the clock'.

One of the longest-serving SAS veterans, who spent a lifetime jumping out of aeroplanes and who still lives in Hereford, had been suffering badly. His knees and ankles were causing him great pain, but he bore the agony with enormous courage. 'Too many hard landings!' he would tell those who tried to help him. Eventually, and after many months of waiting, he underwent a series of operations. After he left hospital he went

245

home on crutches to recover, but was still only able to stagger short distances. One day a few weeks later, he answered the telephone. 'Guess what?' he asked the caller. 'What?' There was a brief pause, and then, with triumph in his gravelly cockney voice, he whispered, 'I've just climbed Pen-Y-Fan!'

Every now and then, the Hereford grapevine buzzes with whispered rumours of recently completed operations or the news that 'they're off again, but we're not sure where . . .' and in the middle of an English winter you may catch a glimpse of someone driving through the county who has an impressive tan, not the sort you can buy on a quick skiing trip to the French Alps. The cast-iron 'loose talk costs lives' rumour-control system that operates in Hereford has been skilfully developed to baffle the simply curious and confuse the media, and it works surprisingly well. It is extremely rare for journalists to penetrate such effective defences, and Fleet Street hardly ever manages to find out anything really interesting until long after it has happened and the SAS men concerned are pruning their roses in retirement. The plethora of soldiers' memoirs, *Bravo Two-Zero*, *The One That Got Away*, and several others, reportedly caused a sensation when they first appeared, but apart from some angry words from veterans who considered McNab and the others were being disloyal and compromising SAS soldiers' security, there was very little attempt by Whitehall to stop publication. It is true that, in the case of McNab's second book, the Ministry of Defence did ask him to alter a few paragraphs for security reasons following an injunction (which he did), but the book still appeared and the publicity surrounding its late arrival undoubtedly boosted its sales.

There are very few countries on earth where the violent exploits of a small group of soldiers fighting in a foreign land would lead to a best-seller and make vast sums of money for those who recount their experiences. So what is the reason for such success and interest in what are essentially old war stories? Is it that the nation is in need of real-life heroes in an age where adventure is increasingly hard to find? The answer is more probably that the reader is just curious to know what makes these men (and women) tick, and why they are prepared to risk their lives fighting wars in hostile, often frighteningly remote parts of the world for very little financial reward. Perhaps the reason they do risk their lives has something to do with patriotism, but most SAS men would probably dismiss that suggestion with a wide grin, reminding you that it is your turn to buy a round of drinks.

CONCLUSION

So does today's so-called civilized world need elite military forces like the SAS who, at the whim of a politician, can be called on to search out and destroy its enemies? There are a multitude of examples in history where the existence of elite groups has led to the destruction of societies and occasionally entire civilizations, Hitler's Third Reich being one of them. Is today's world a more dangerous place than it was in other centuries, or is it that with modern communications and constant live news updates available at the touch of a remote-control television button we have learned to witness and accept the dangers that surround us, dangers which our ancestors never saw? It is most unlikely that there will be lasting peace in every corner of this planet in the next decade or even the next century. Until there is peace, therefore, perhaps we really do need experts to protect us.

Karl von Clausewitz's observation that 'War is nothing more than the continuation of policy by other means' has been proved right numerous times this century, and there is no evidence today that the future will be brighter. How far a democracy can allow a force like the SAS to go on protecting the nation's interests is, however, a matter of conjecture. As long as the aggression for which the Regiment has become renowned is controlled by a democratically elected government there would appear to be little danger. Problems only arise when that aggression is turned against the people that such forces are supposed to be defending, as can be seen in countries where death squads roam the streets.

The fact that SAS men do not go around cold-bloodedly murdering suspects or captives, or even the innocent, can be proved by looking closely at the facts. If they had chosen to do so, hundreds of Provisional IRA gunmen and bombers would have been summarily executed by the SAS in Northern Ireland and in their safe havens south of the border over the last two decades or so. For years rumours have abounded accusing SAS teams of having executed their enemies, but there is absolutely no proof that this has ever happened. In every anti-terrorist operation there are risks to passers-by, and innocent members of the public have in the past been mistaken for gunmen or bombers, or have been caught in crossfire, but such tragedies will, inevitably, always occur in a guerrilla war.

If we accept the idea that armed force is sometimes required either for our own protection or as a method of suppressing violence against our friends and allies, we could not wish for a more dependable force than the SAS. When the chips are down, an irresolute and indecisive soldier who runs away when his life is on the line is of little use to anyone. As General Sir John Hackett puts it: 'The success of armies depends to a very high degree on the coherence of the group, and the coherence of the group depends on the degree of trust and confidence of its members in each other.' Members of Britain's 22 Special Air Service Regiment have maintained that tradition of confidence ever since their predecessors first took their lives in their hands and leapt out of a Bristol Bombay over the Western Desert on the night of 16 November 1941. The fact that we have today in the United Kingdom professional and effective armed forces capable of defending our country and our people is surely something for which we should be grateful.

GLOSSARY

ASU	Active Service Unit
ATO	Ammunition Technical Officer
Black Ops	operations where blue-black Nomex fire-retardant overalls and body armour is worn
BMP	Soviet-bloc armoured personnel carrier
CIA	Central Intelligence Agency
CO	commanding officer
COBRA	Cabinet Office Briefing Room
CQB	Close Quarter Battle
CRW	counter-revolutionary warfare
cut-off(s)	armed group(s) placed on perimeter of ambush site
DET	The Detachment – 14th Intelligence and Security Company; also known as 14 Int.
DMSU	Divisional Mobile Support Unit of the RUC
DPM	disruptive pattern material
DS	Directing Staff
ELINT	electronic intelligence
E4	operations unit of RUC Special Branch
E4A	covert surveillance unit of RUC Special Branch
GPMG	7.62mm general-purpose machine gun ('gimpy')
Garda Síochána	the police force of the Republic of Ireland
Green Ops	operations in DPM combat fatigues
GPS	global positioning systems
HAHO	high altitude high opening
HALO	high altitude low opening
Headshed	SAS commanding officer and staff at HQ Hereford
HMSU	Headquarters Mobile Support Unit (RUC)
HUMINT	human intelligence
INLA	Irish National Liberation Army

JIC	Joint Intelligence Committee
JOC	Joint Operations Centre
killing area	target area of an ambush
LUP	lying-up position
MRF	Mobile Reconnaissance Force
MSR	Main Supply Route
MI5	Security Service
MI6	Secret Intelligence Service
M203	40mm grenade launcher often attached to M16 rifle
NCO	non-commissioned officer
OP	observation post
PIRA	Provisional Irish Republican Army
PLCE	personal load-carriage equipment
PNV	passive night vision
RTU	returned to unit
RUC	Royal Ulster Constabulary
RV	rendezvous
SA-80	5.56mm automatic standard-issue army rifle
SBS	Special Boat Service (Royal Marines)
SIGINT	signals intelligence
sitrep	situation report
Snuffbox	Security Service (MI5)
SP team	Special Projects (CRW) Team
SPG	Special Patrol Group
TACBE	tactical distress beacon
TCG	Tasking and Co-ordination Group
UDA	Ulster Defence Association
UNPROFOR	United Nations Protection Force
UDR	Ulster Defence Regiment
UVF	Ulster Volunteer Force
VCP	vehicle checkpoint
windproof	SAS-issue lightweight DPM combat smock

INDEX